Religions and Beliefs

Series Editor: Ina Taylor

Christianity

Ina Taylor

Nelson Thornes

a Wolters Kluwer business

Published in 2006 by:
Nelson Thornes Ltd
Delta Place
27 Bath Road
CHELTENHAM
GL53 7TH
United Kingdom

06 07 08 09 10 / 10 9 8 7 6 5 4 3 2 1

A catalogue record for this book is available from the British Library

ISBN 0 7487 9670 3

Edited by Judi Hunter
Picture research by Sue Sharp
Illustrations by Tom Barnfield, Angela Lumley, Richard Morris, Harry Venning
Page make-up by eMC Design

Printed in Croatia by Zrinski

Acknowledgements

With thanks to the following for permission to reproduce photographs and other copyright material in this book:

Cover photo: imagebroker/ Alamy

A Rocha UK: 106A; Peter Adams/ Digital Vision BP (NT): 105C; Advertising Archive: 57C; Alamy/ David Hoffman Photo Library: 107C; Alamy/ Jack Carey: 90/91A; Alamy/ Janine Wiedel: 28A, 72A; Alamy/ Manor Photography: 10A; Alamy/ Natural History Museum: 101 (top); Alamy/ Photofusion: 76A; Alpha International: 48 (right); Amnesty International: 83B; Andes Press Agency/ Carlos Reyes- Manzo: 110A; ARC: 110B; ArkReligion.com/ Viesti Collection: 59B; Art Directors & Trip Photolibrary/ ArkReligion.com: 13B, 15B, 17B, 28B, 58A, 66 (top right), 81C; Art Archive/ Bibliothèque Municipale Poitiers/ Dagli Orti: 62A; Bananastock P (NT): 55 (right); John Birdsall Photography: 7D, 54A, 125E; Bridgeman Art Library/ Jesus Returning the Keys to St. Peter, 1820 (oil on canvas), Ingres, Jean Auguste Dominique (1780-1867)/ Musee Ingres, Montauban, France, Lauros/ Giraudon: 33C; Bridgeman Art Library/ Virgin and Child (oil on panel), Greek School, (16th century)/ Church of San Martino, Venice, Italy, Cameraphoto Arte Venezia: 25B; British Humanist Association: 9B; Christian Aid/ Louise Orton: 97B; Church Housing Trust and English Churches Housing Group: 94 (all); Circa Photo Library/ Mas de Solan Community: 111D; Corbis/ Anna Clopet: 36/37A; Corbis/ Archivo Iconografico, S.A.: 21B; Corbis/ David Turnley: 45 (background); Corbis/ Filip Schulke: 77D; Corbis/ Peter Schouten/ National Geographic Society/ Reuters: 43C; Corbis/ Peter Turnley: 82 (top left), 86 (top left), 88A, 126; Corbis/ Reuters: 116A; Corbis/ Sygma: 35B ; Corbis/ Touhig Sion/ Sygma: 121B; Corbis GS V94 (NT): 18A; Corel 799 (NT): 76C; Digital Vision 15 (NT): 85, 101 (bottom); Empics/ AP: 14A, 100 (top right); Empics/ PA: 65B, 119B; Empics/ Rangers FC: 38A; Eularia Clarke, 'Storm over the Lake', from the Methodist Church Collection of Modern Christian Art Copyright: Trustees for Methodist Church Purposes, used by permission of Trustees of the Collection: 44; Christian International Peace Service: 123A; ffotograff Photolibrary & Agency: 16A, 66 (bottom right); Getty Images: 26A, 95, 84, 100 (bottom), 114 (left), 118A, 121C; Antony Gormley EUROPEAN FIELD 1993 Terracotta variable size: approx. 40 000 figures, each 8-26 cm high – courtesy of the artist and Jay Jopling/ White Cube: 8A; Greenpeace UK: 103; Housing Justice: 74A, 75B (Attribution for prayer on page 75: adapted from 'The Trampled Vineyard', www.housingjustice.org.uk), 75C; Impact Photos/ Mark Henley: 18B; John Lawrence: 70B; Kidz Klub Liverpool: 71C; MegaBite: 73B and C; Mirrorpix/ Austin Hargrave: 80A; National Gallery Picture Library: 61D; Barbara Penoyar/ Photodisc 16 (NT): 24A, 54 (bottom left); Kevin Peterson/ Photodisc 33 (NT): 6B; Photofusion: 60A, 64A; Photofusion/ Libby Welsh: 66 (middle); Photofusion/ Peter Olive: 67 (bottom); PYMCA/ Paul Hartnett: 48 (left); Rex Features/ Action Press: 40A; Rex Features/ Alex Segre: 108A; Rex Features/ Alistair Linford: 81B; Rex Features/ Dave Allocca: 89B; Rex Features/ Sipa Press: 34A, 68/69C; Rim Light/ Photolink/ Photodisc 32 (NT): 31C; Antonia Rolls: 32A; RSPCA Photo Library: 45 (middle left); Sally & Richard Greenhill: 6A, 7C, 45 (top and bottom left), 47C, 55 (left), 114 (right), 115 (both); RJL Smith of Much Wenlock: 82A; Sonia Halliday Photography: 11B, 53B; Sonia Halliday Photography/ David Silverman: 17C; Martin Sookias: 5, 51B, 52A; Stocktrek/ Photodisc 44 (NT): 120A; Ina Taylor: 22A, 27B, 63B, 102A, 111C; Tearfund: 76B; Topfoto: 79A; Topfoto/ UPPA/ Richard Harding/ Starstock/ Photoshot: 69D; Week of Prayer for World Peace: 124A; Y Care International: 98,99 (all).

Scriptures are taken from the Good News Bible published by The Bible Societies/Collins © American Bible Society.

Extract on page 20 adapted from article © Bryan Appleyard/ The Sunday Times/ 13 March 2005, and reproduced with permission.

Extract on page 25, from Faith in Conservation: New Approaches to Religions and the Environment by Martin Palmer and Victoria Finlay © The World Bank, Washington DC, 2003, p56, reproduced with kind permission.

Quote from Dr John Polkinghorne on page 41 reproduced with kind permission.

Direct quotes on page 38 from 'Rangers centre-back whose game rests on divine intervention' The Guardian, 21 May 2005 © Guardian Newspapers Limited 2005, and on page 71 from 'Missionary takes on tough test in darkest Telford', The Guardian, 11 July 2005 © Guardian Newspapers Limited 2005, reproduced with permission of The Guardian.

Extracts on pages 48–49 reproduced from Alpha News 'The War Cry', 19 February 2005, and reproduced with permission of Alpha News and Jo Reynolds.

Material on 'marriage' (pages 58–59) from the Church of England website is copyright © The Archbishops' Council, 2004; Material from 'The Marriage Service', Common Worship: Services and Prayers for the Church of England: Pastoral Services is copyright © The Archbishops' Council, 2000.

With thanks to the Salvation Army for permission to reproduce the extract on page 64.

With thanks to Tearfund for permission to reproduce material on pages 76–77; the quote on page 77 from the Tearfund Youth Website, 2004 © Tearfund 2004, and reproduced with permission.

With thanks to Christian Aid for permission to reproduce material on pages 76–77, 80–81, 96–97. Material on pages 80–81 reproduced with kind permission of Christian Aid and Ronan Keating, from Christian Aid Newsletter (Autumn 2004). Material on pages 96–97 reproduced with kind permission of Christian Aid, from Christian Aid Newsletter (Autumn 2000).

With thanks to Amnesty International and also to ACAT (Action by Christians Against Torture, www.acatuk.org.uk) for permission to reproduce material on pages 82–83.

Extract on page 91 adapted from article © Christopher Morgan/ The Times/ 6 February 2005, and reproduced with permission.

'I was Hungry' poem and artwork (92A) from Whose World? reproduced from the front cover of Christian Ecology Link's pamphlet 'Justice, Peace and Sustainable Living'.

Extracts on page 93B and on page 105 from Sharing God's Planet (Church House Publishing, 2005) is copyright © The Archbishops' Council, 2005.

Extract from the Orthodox Christian Church on page 93, from the article 'Introduction to Christian Environmental Initiatives' by Martin Palmer, The Greek Orthodox Archdiocese of America website (www.goarch.org).

Extract 102B reproduced with kind permission of the British Humanist Association (www.humanism.org.uk).

Greenpeace campaign leaflet (103C) reproduced with kind permission of Greenpeace.

Eco-Congregation Prayer 105B from the Bethesda Methodist Church website (www.bethesda-church.org.uk).

Quote from Padre Langston on page 119 reproduced from the article 'A man of God in the army', with kind permission of BBC News at bbcnews.com.

Quote from CAFOD on page 121 reproduced with kind permission.

Every effort has been made to contact copyright holders and we apologise if any have been overlooked.

Contents

 # Fast facts about Christianity

Q When did it begin?

Christianity began around 2,000 years ago when Jesus was born in the country we now call Israel. Like Judaism and Islam, Christianity grew out of the earlier life and teachings of the prophet Abraham.

Q What is Christianity?

Christianity is the name of the religion followed by Christians. It is based on the life and teachings of Jesus.

Q Types of Christianity

There are thousands of different types of Christianity. Most of these are within three groups: Roman Catholicism; Eastern Orthodoxy; and Protestantism. Although they share the same fundamental belief in the teachings of Jesus, the Son of God, they have different ways of worshipping and slightly different interpretations of things. Approximately half of the world's Christians are Roman Catholic.

The author of this book is a Quaker, which is a small Protestant group.

Q How many Christians are there today?

There are around two billion Christians in the world today. At over 30% of the world's population, that makes Christianity the world's largest religion. In the UK there are around 41 million people who identify themselves as Christian, which also makes it the largest religion in the UK.

Looking for meaning

> I think life is a bit like a jigsaw puzzle. You have been given all the pieces and you have got to find how they fit together. The only problem is you haven't got the picture to help you!

One of the things that makes us superior to other animals is the fact that we ask questions. As humans, we keep trying to make sense of life. It is automatic almost. If you saw a policeman walk into school this morning, you would wonder why he had come. You would also probably think of a couple of possible reasons for him being there. It's true a dog would immediately notice someone different arriving, but it is unlikely that a dog, no matter how intelligent, would consider various reasons for the person being there.

It is all questions!

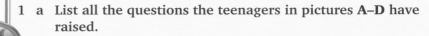

objective

to understand what an ultimate question is

glossary

Big Bang
Conscience
Evolution
Tsunami
Ultimate question

Activity

1 a List all the questions the teenagers in pictures **A–D** have raised.

  b Choose *one* of their questions and suggest what answers could be offered? Would you agree with any of those answers?

2 Draw your own speech bubble and write *three* questions inside that you would like to know the answer to.

> There are some things I just can't get my head around. I mean what's the point of me being here? I don't just mean in this room, but on this planet and now. You can't tell me that something as highly developed as a human being happened by accident. If that was true, all sorts of weird things would be appearing everywhere and at any time. Well, they don't. So what am I here for?

> I want to know why some things go horribly wrong and innocent people suffer. Remember that terrible **tsunami** in 2004, when thousands and thousands of people were killed and injured? People didn't deserve that, did they? Okay, I suppose there were a few evil people who got hurt, but that still doesn't justify it.

Beliefs and concepts

6

None of the questions these teenagers asked had easy answers. They are often referred to as **ultimate questions** because they are concerned with the meaning of life. These are questions that do not have a right or a wrong answer. In fact it is often impossible to be sure whether there will be an answer to them at all. They may concern things you can't prove. But one thing is certain, most people will have an opinion on the subject!

Activity

3 Look back to the questions in your speech bubble. Are any of them ultimate questions?

4 a Read the questions below and sort them into two lists: those that could be answered; and those that are ultimate questions.
   - What time is 'EastEnders' on tonight?
   - Is there a God?
   - Who is the Prime Minister?
   - What will happen to my mind after I have died?
   - Do you only live on earth once?
   - How many pupils are there in the school?
   - Is it going to rain today?

   b Add *two* more ordinary questions and *two* more ultimate questions to your lists. You can either use two of the teenagers' ultimate questions or add some of your own.

5 What do people usually mean when they say, 'That's one of life's little mysteries'? What situation might produce this type of comment? Do you think it is possible that life does have mysteries we will never be able to understand? Why?

What really intrigues me is the scientific stuff. I want to know about the beginning of the universe. Oh yes, I go along with the **Big Bang** and **evolution** and all that sort of thing, but why did it start? What was there before? Now that's the really mind-boggling stuff for me!

I want to know if I'm free to do what I like. Well, why not? What's stopping me? Yes, I know I've got a **conscience** but where did that come from? Anyway, who says something is right or wrong?

Where do we look for answers?

objective

to consider where people look for help with problems

glossary

Agnostic
Atheist
Humanist

Have you got the answer? Ask yourself!

We often turn to ourselves first to see if we can make sense of something. That is not surprising. We have got the best brain in the animal kingdom and we gain experience as we grow older. If you add to that the amazing technology we have developed during the past decade, it is not surprising that most of us can solve problems our great-grandparents never dreamt of.

More help needed?

All too often we find that we can't solve everything on our own. As we have already discovered, most of the ultimate questions that appeared on pages 6–7 proved impossible to answer. Does that mean that we have got to get outside help? Are these the sort of questions that need help from a higher intelligence?

Some people would answer 'yes' to all those questions. They are convinced that no matter how intelligent humans become, they will never possess the phenomenal power of God. For these people, religion is the only way to get the help they need when searching for answers to difficult questions.

Although there are many world religions and they appear very different, they are actually very similar. Each religion gives its followers help and guidance with problem solving. People aren't left helplessly on their own. Instead, they are shown ways of seeking help from a higher power. That higher power is God.

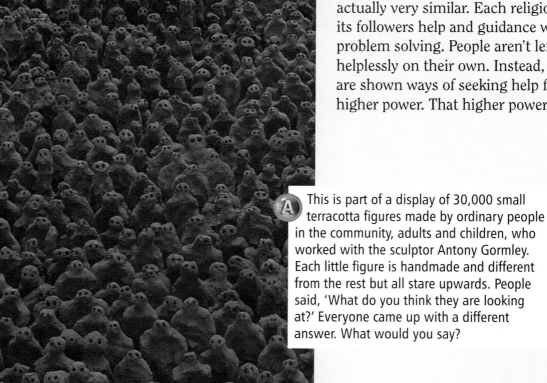

(A) This is part of a display of 30,000 small terracotta figures made by ordinary people in the community, adults and children, who worked with the sculptor Antony Gormley. Each little figure is handmade and different from the rest but all stare upwards. People said, 'What do you think they are looking at?' Everyone came up with a different answer. What would you say?

Beliefs and concepts

Where Christians get help

This book studies the way in which Christianity helps people to find answers to the difficult questions in life. Christians believe that God not only created everything, including people, but that he cares for them. As a sign of his love for humanity, God sent his son Jesus to earth to help people. By studying the teachings of Jesus and following the example he set, Christians believe they gain help in solving the difficult problems of life.

Not everyone believes in the existence of God. **Atheists** are people who are certain God doesn't exist. Other people, called **agnostics**, are less sure. They say there may be a god but we will never be able to prove it because we are only human and our brain is not powerful enough to deal with such difficult concepts.

One group of people who do not believe religion helps them to answer difficult questions are the **Humanists**. They reject religion because they say more evidence is necessary before they can believe anything. For them, the evidence has to be scientific data or something that can be seen with their own eyes. They also point out that some questions may not actually have any answers. Do you think this is possible?

Would you extend this argument to brain power? Do you think there are some things that we will never be able to understand because we are human?

1 Write down *three* things you believe but know you can't possibly prove.

2 Some people who saw the exhibition of little clay figures in picture **A** thought it was meant to be religious. Why would they think that? In fact Antony Gormley, the sculptor, denied that it had a religious message.

B This is the international symbol of Humanism. It was originally designed as a logo for the British Humanist Association, but is now recognised around the world as the symbol of Humanism. It is often called the 'happy human'. Besides looking like a capital H, what else does their logo remind you of? How do you think this fits in with the idea that we should come up with answers based on evidence and reasoning?

3 When you can't come up with the answer to a problem yourself, what other problem solvers do you turn to? List at least *three*. Against each, write down the types of questions they are best at answering.

4 Many people would say that humans will never be able to fly like birds without the aid of a machine. With a partner, decide on *four* other things which you think human beings will never be able to do because of the way they are built. See if the rest of the class agrees with you.

Who are Christians?

Christianity is recognised as a major world faith and the main religion in Britain. The most recent census in 2001 revealed 72% of British people (41 million) described themselves as Christian. Surprised? The census form did have a box for 'no religion' and 15% of the population chose to tick that box, which made non-believers the second-largest group of people in the country, more than followers of all the other world faiths. So, although people might say, 'Nobody believes in that God and Jesus stuff nowadays,' it is not true.

Figures for church attendance are very low but that is only one part of being a Christian. Plenty of people call themselves Christian because they accept Christian beliefs and values even though they never go to church.

A New churches are still being built in the twenty-first century. This one is under construction in Swindon, Wiltshire.

> **Activity**
> 1 As a class, discuss why most people in Britain call themselves Christian but don't go to church?
>
> 2 Which do you think matters most, what you believe in or what you actually do? Why?

What unites Christians around the world?

Not surprisingly for such a large worldwide group, there are differences in the way some Christians worship, although they regard themselves as one strong body. Some of the different Christian groups you might have heard of are Methodists, Anglicans, Baptists, Roman Catholics, Salvation Army, Quakers and Baptists. These are only a few different branches of Christianity. They are united by their belief in **Jesus** Christ, which is obvious from their name! Christians believe Jesus was an extraordinary person who taught humanity a good way to live.

Christians also believe that Jesus was the son of God who was born to a human mother. This makes him unique because he was partly human and partly divine. As such, he was able to bring God's message directly to people and teach it in a way they could understand. Because Jesus lived alongside people on earth, he could show them what to do by his example. Christians also believe that Jesus is their **saviour**; this means God sent him to save people from the consequences of their sins.

Christians also believe that Jesus was killed because of his beliefs, then miraculously brought back to life three days later by God. Jesus only remained on earth in bodily form for a further few weeks before he went to heaven. Christians believe that, although Jesus' bodily presence went, his divine presence remained on earth and is still here today. The spiritual Jesus is here to guide anyone who asks for help. They believe Jesus does help people but not always in the way they expect. Some Christians believe they get help through prayer or through studying holy scriptures. At other times, people can be helped through the kindness of fellow human beings who have been inspired by God. For some Christians, assistance comes to them in miraculous ways which seem to challenge the rules of science.

For most Christians, believing in the divine and supernatural power of Jesus is an essential part of their faith. It is one of the reasons why they are convinced there is life after death.

B Believing in Jesus and following his teachings is what unites Christians around the world. Christianity is an international religion with 2.2 billion followers making it the largest world religion.

Activity

3 Consider these ways people have thought about worldwide Christianity.

   a One person said Christianity is like a vase of different flowers which are all lovely in their own right. They look beautiful together and all draw life from the same water.

   b Another person thought Christians were like the fingers in a glove. Each is different and can work independently but they are all connected to the same strong centre. When they work together they are very powerful.

   Choose *one* of these images above, or your own idea, and make a design for a T-shirt that young Christians could wear to show they are united.

4 Write a paragraph explaining what Christians think about Jesus.

What do Christians believe God is like?

objective

to examine different Christian beliefs about God

glossary

Gospels
Omnipotent
Omniscient
Trinity

A What sort of questions does this humorous sticker raise? Do you think it would make any difference to people's ideas about God if God was referred to as 'she'?

Christians believe there is only one God who knows everything that is happening in the world; everything that happened in the past and everything that will happen in the future. Someone who knows everything is called **omniscient**. This comes from two Latin words.

Omnis = all and *sciens* = knowledge.

Christians also believe that God has existed forever. He has no beginning and will never end. God is eternal.

God is also **omnipotent**, which comes from another Latin word. *Omnis* = all and *potens* = powerful, so God is more powerful than anything in existence.

Any one of these beliefs is really difficult to understand because nothing exists for us to compare it with. For some Christians, that is where their belief rests. They are convinced there is a power that is greater than us, that cares about us, but these Christians say we can't really imagine a being like that with our limited human brains.

Other Christians are sure that Jesus left people with sufficient information which has been written down in the **Gospels** for us to have a good understanding of God. Because of the different ways Jesus referred to God, Christians have found it easier to think in terms of God as the **Trinity**.

- As a father who created everything in existence and still looks after it. He has a caring attitude towards his creation. God the Father.
- As having a human face in Jesus living the life of a person on earth. God the Son who can save people from their sins.
- As a spirit who is an invisible, but powerful, presence alive in the world today helping people. God the Holy Spirit.

The idea of something having three parts, but essentially being one thing, is a difficult concept to imagine. A favourite symbol is that of the clover leaf made up of three leaf segments. Another is of water which can also appear as ice or steam depending on the conditions; but is still the same thing.

God is traditionally referred to as 'He' but that is not because Christians believe God is male. Indeed, Christians believe God has no gender because that is an earthly concept. However, it seems rude and disrespectful to refer to any being as 'it' and so God is usually referred to as 'He' in Christianity.

Activity

1   Draw an image of something which is made up of three parts but is essentially one object. Then label it with the Christian ideas of the Trinity.

2   What sort of characteristics do you think the three aspects of God might have? How might a father-figure regard his followers? How could the human side of God help people? What would the Holy Spirit be able to do for modern Christians?

3   Would it make any difference to Christian ideas about God if people referred to God as a mother rather than a father-figure?

B One branch of Christianity is called the Orthodox. The sign of the cross they make when praying gives an understanding about their belief in God. Three fingers touch the forehead first to ask God to be in their mind and to bless their thoughts.
The hand then moves to touch the chest to ask God to put love in the person's heart.
The hand next touches the right shoulder, then the left, to ask a blessing for the deeds of the hands. Some Orthodox Christians also bow and touch the ground to remind themselves that God created humans from the earth.

The first two fingers come together to touch the thumb.

These three fingers remind the Christian there is one God who is three persons – God the Father, God the Son and God the Holy Spirit.

The other two fingers are held close to the palm and remind the worshipper of the two aspects of Jesus. One finger is for Jesus as the Son of God and the other for Jesus as a human being.

Activity

4   Use the information in **B** to write a paragraph about the beliefs of Orthodox Christians.

5   Christians say God is at the centre of their life. What difference do you think this makes to the way they behave?

6   Some Christians have said it would be more accurate to refer to God as a mother-figure rather than a father-figure. What reasons could they give for this? Would you agree?

objective

to look at Christian beliefs about people and their relationship with God

glossary

Bible
Redeem
Redemption
Steward

What do Christians believe about people?

Are we just animals?

Koko is a 34-year-old gorilla who has been the focus of some interesting experiments in America. She has lived with the scientist Dr Penny Patterson for 33 of those years, during which time Koko has been treated as much like a human child as possible. She has been taught sign language and can now sign 1,000 words, but she actually understands about 2,000. It means she can hold simple conversations with humans by putting between three and six words together. The reason Koko cannot speak words is because gorillas do not have the same voice-boxes as humans. She has, however, been taught to use a keyboard linked to a voice synthesizer which can create the sound of a human voice.

A Which would you say is the more intelligent animal in this picture? Why?

1 Do you think it is fair to train animals to do things like Koko? It is clear that gorillas are very intelligent animals. Should we treat them as equals? Why?

2 What question would you like to e-mail to Koko?

Humans created in God's image

Christians do not believe animals are equal to human beings. The creation stories in the **Bible** speak of God creating animal life and then later creating human beings. The Bible also says:

'…God created human beings, making them to be like himself.'

(Genesis 1:27)

All of this leads Christians to believe that humans are more important than animals. The passage about being 'like himself' is thought to mean people are capable of growing closer to God not that people actually look like God. Whilst animals like Koko are an important part of God's creation, Christians would say humans are the superior breed. They are the highest form of God's creation.

Although humans have a special place in God's creation, Christians believe they also have responsibilities. It is their duty to care for the planet and the rest of God's creation, including other animals. Christians think of themselves as **stewards** of the earth. Stewards and stewardesses on an aeroplane are in control of the smooth running of life in the cabin of the plane. It is their duty to look after the needs and comfort of their passengers, but, ultimately, the cabin crew come under the total control of the plane's captain.

 According to the Bible, humans were the pinnacle of God's creation.

What's so special about people?

Christians believe that, as the highest form of creation, they have a special relationship with God, their creator. This means they must live their lives in such a way that they draw nearer to God. To do this, they need to communicate with God in various ways. It might be through worship or personal prayer when they can open their mind to God.

Christians believe God came to earth in the human form of Jesus. Because he was both man and God, Jesus was able to teach people about their relationship with God. The Bible says that early man sinned and humans became separated from God who had created them. The arrival of Jesus changed all that. Here was someone who was prepared to sacrifice his earthly life to **redeem** people from their sins. This meant that people could be saved from eternal punishment and have everlasting life with God instead. Christians do not think animals have received this special gift of **redemption** from God.

> **Activity**
>
> 3 On a large sheet of paper draw the outlines of a human and an animal. Within the human outline, list some characteristics that show humans are superior to animals. In the animal outline, list some characteristics that animals possess which humans do not.
>
> 4 'We are just animals.' Why don't Christians agree with this? What do you think?
>
> 5 Write your answer to the question: 'What do Christians believe about people?'

Communicating with God

glossary

Crucifix
Holy Communion
Liturgy
Meditation
Prayer
Roman Catholic
Transubstantiation

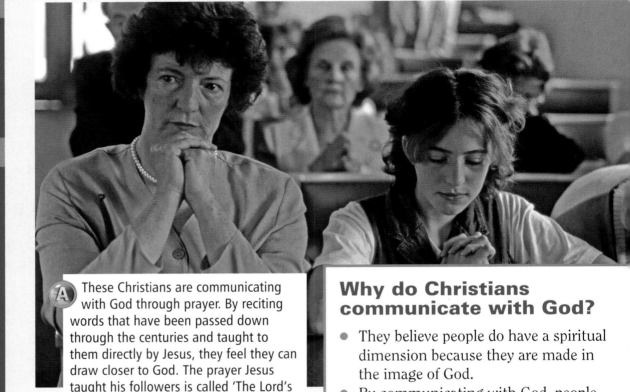

(A) These Christians are communicating with God through prayer. By reciting words that have been passed down through the centuries and taught to them directly by Jesus, they feel they can draw closer to God. The prayer Jesus taught his followers is called 'The Lord's Prayer' and begins 'Our Father who art in heaven'.

Why do Christians communicate with God?

- They believe people do have a spiritual dimension because they are made in the image of God.
- By communicating with God, people can draw closer to God.

1   Look up 'The Lord's Prayer' in Matthew 6:9–15. Copy it out. Use a different coloured pen to underline: where Christians are asking for something; where they are saying thank you; where they are praising God; where they are saying sorry and asking for forgiveness.

2   Why do you think Christians find this is the most useful prayer they have?

Prayer for a Christian can be a group activity like the one shown in picture **A** or something very personal. Group prayer is helpful because Christians can draw strength from each other, as well as from contact with God. A set prayer used by a group is called a **liturgy** and many Christians find this a good way of communicating with God because reciting well-known words can focus the mind.

B

Some Christians find it easier to communicate with God quietly and on their own. The person in picture **B** is meditating. This means they are simply thinking about God and keeping their mind open to any thoughts God puts there. Some people like to have an object to focus their thoughts on. This Christian has chosen to begin by looking at a **crucifix** which will concentrate their mind on the sacrifice Jesus made for her. Others prefer to read a passage from the Bible then think about it. Some begin by looking at a religious picture. Many people close their eyes after a while so they can concentrate better. Those who choose **meditation** as a way of communicating with God like it because it is very personal. They can share whatever is in their mind with God and open their hearts to God's response.

- God will help people through life. God will support them in difficult times, comfort them when they are suffering and guide them through life.
- Being close to God is the whole purpose of life. A Christian would feel something was missing in their life if they were not in touch with God.

Sometimes communication with God comes totally out of the blue. For one 16-year-old the experience was life-changing. Hugh Montefiore, from a well-known Jewish family, was sitting at his desk doing his homework when he had a vision of Jesus. Much to the consternation of his family, Hugh converted to Christianity, then studied Christianity at university, became a priest and eventually a bishop. Other Christians have experienced revelations like this. For some, the experience of God has come in a dream, or in a crisis when they have been faced with a life-threatening situation like a road accident or a serious illness. Like Hugh Montefiore, they have been so sure of God's presence it has changed their life.

Activity

3 a What are Christians using to focus their thoughts on God in each of the pictures?

b What connection does each have with the person of Jesus?

c Which do you think a new Christian would find the easiest way of communicating with God? Why is this?

Some Christians feel closest to God when taking part in the service of mass or **Holy Communion**. The ceremony involves eating a piece of bread (usually a wafer) and taking a sip of wine to remind Christians of the bread and wine Jesus had during his last meal on earth. This leads them to think of how Jesus gave his life to save people from death. Some Christians, such as **Roman Catholics**, believe that during the ceremony the bread mystically changes into the body of Christ and the wine into his blood. This is called **transubstantiation**. Those who take part in the mass feel they become spiritually very close to Jesus. Other Christians do not believe the bread and wine changes, but they still think taking part in the ritual of Holy Communion enables them to communicate better with God.

C Receiving Holy Communion, the bread and wine, brings Christians closer to God.

17

It's all in the mind – or is it?

objective

to review what other dimensions might exist

glossary

Guardian angel
Paranormal
Reincarnation
Soul
Spirit
Spiritual

> What else do you need to know so that you really feel you know me? List the different pieces of information you would need. Would it help if I gave you my chemical make-up? Does that define me? Would a model of my DNA, or my fingerprint, help?

A

1 What do you think is vital to knowing someone? How necessary is it to know their personality, sense of humour, kindness, sarcasm, bad habits? What else would you list here that would define the person? Is there any way you can measure any of these aspects of a person?

Activity

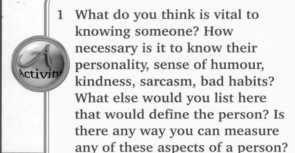

B The mind is separate from the body and it is very powerful. This is not a trick picture. This man has used the power of his mind to overcome the feelings of pain his body is experiencing.

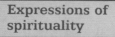

2 Name *three* other examples of mind over matter. Do you think animals have this ability? Does it prove there is another dimension to human existence?

3 Conduct a survey of your year group to find out what percentage believes in the paranormal.

Another dimension?

A recent survey in Britain showed that 70% of people believe something more exists than we can see with our own eyes. Some people think it is possible for certain humans to possess an awareness of another dimension, something **paranormal**. It might involve seeing ghosts or believing they can communicate with the dead. For others, it might take the form of visions of holy people, or a belief that they have received a special message from God.

● Do you think people have to believe in God to believe in another dimension? Why?

What do they think?

Although most of the following ideas are not recognised as official beliefs by the Christian Church, they are still quite popular ideas amongst the 70% of the population who think there is a **spiritual** dimension to life. You may think some are possible yourself. It is also likely you will have seen films or read stories based on the ideas. Does it make them true? Not necessarily. In the end, it all comes down to what you believe and what sort of proof you are looking for.

A few people think they have lived on earth before. This is called **reincarnation**. They say they can remember being a person who lived in the past and can often give names of people and places they knew in their former life. The thread that links them from the past to present, and possibly into the future, is a **spirit** not a body.

Others believe that after they die, there is a part of them that continues to exist. This is not bodily either, it is a spirit. Christians call this their **soul**.

Some are sure there are spirits that watch over the living and generally protect them from harm. These spirits are referred to as **guardian angels**.

There are cases of people who have suffered from illnesses which medical science has said are incurable. Their strong belief in a greater power than humanity has, in some instances, helped them to fully recover.

Some people who believe that humans are the highest form of creation argue that we have a spiritual dimension. It is certainly true that we possess powers that other animals do not, and many of these powers are connected with the mind. We have the ability to react to the wonders of nature. We respond to a piece of artwork like sculpture, music or painting in a totally different way to an animal. Our emotions and our sense of humour are all essentially human characteristics that distinguish us from animals.

4 You have been asked to send *three* questions to a chat show. The host is going to interview the man lying on a bed of nails in picture B. What would you like to ask him?

5 Take *one* of the supernatural phenomena mentioned on these pages and write down a possible 'natural' explanation of the event.

6 Make a list of the points for and against the existence of another dimension. Would you say it was all in the mind? Or do you think humans might have a spiritual dimension in some form?

'I'm going to live forever'

Everybody wants to live forever but nobody wants to get old.

objective

to examine different attitudes towards everlasting life

glossary

Apparition
Hallucination
Supernatural

Activity

1 a What sort of things can people do to their bodies in the twenty-first century to prevent themselves looking old? The adverts in **A** will give you some ideas.

   b If you were middle-aged, would you make yourself look younger? Why? What are the advantages and disadvantages of appearing younger than you are?

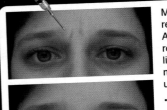

EVERLASTING LIFE!

Cambridge scientist Aubrey de Grey believes that young people alive today under the age of 11 could live forever. Well, if not forever, then at least until they are 1,200 years old! De Grey says two-thirds of us die of old age, so if we could cure that, people would just live on and on and on… The way to do it, he says, is through stem cell therapy. Basically, our organs would continually be renewed before they became worn out.

Er, forgotten it
The only problem is even if our bodies could last 1,000 years our memory wouldn't cope. We would only be able to remember a third of what had happened to us. So what? Most of us can't remember much about being two years old.

Bit crowded here!
Another problem is that the world is likely to get a bit crowded with all us happy 800-year-olds running around. So we will probably have to choose between having a baby and living forever. You can't do both, there won't be enough space!

(Adapted from 'I'm going to live forever' *The Sunday Times*, 13 March 2005)

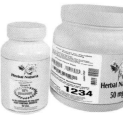

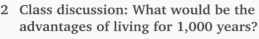

2 Class discussion: What would be the advantages of living for 1,000 years?
- Would there be any disadvantages?
- What effect do you think it would have on our society?
- Could you have a large number of artificial stem cell replacements and remain the same person?

 This is the death-mask of the pharaoh Tutankhamun.

Belief in life after death has been around almost as long as people have. This beautiful death-mask covered the Egyptian mummy of Tutankhamun. The contents of his pyramid show people believed in life after death more than 3,000 years ago. Dishes of food, flagons of wine, pieces of furniture and models of servants prove the Egyptians thought life would carry on after death much like this life.

Humanists believe we only live once. They say life is not a 'dress-rehearsal' for anything else and, because this is the only life we have, it is very precious. They think the only way we will continue after we have died is in people's memories, or through our children or possibly as a result of things we have done in our lifetime.

We won't totally disappear either. The molecules that make up our bodies will still continue to exist as particles in the natural world long after our bodies have gone.

Supernatural experiences

Some people who do not have any religious beliefs are still convinced there is life after death. It is often because they have experienced something they cannot explain. It might be a **supernatural** or ghostly experience where they have seen an **apparition** of someone they know is dead. There is a difference in the way people have reported experiencing spirits. Some say they hear their presence, others see them and for some it is just a feeling that there is a supernatural presence near them. For these people, their experience is evidence of another world beyond this one. There are of course plenty of people who say it is all in their imagination!

There are interesting reports of people who have had near-death experiences. They have 'died' on the operating table for a brief time before being revived. These people tell similar stories of seeing a light at the end of a tunnel and they were moving towards it before they were brought back to life.

Do you think either of these experiences are evidence of life after death? Or are they just **hallucinations**?

3 Write a short piece for a Humanist magazine explaining why some people argue that human life is more valuable if you do not believe in life after death.

4 Role-play a radio phone-in with a person who claims to have had a near-death experience.

Whatever next?

A Last year's dead leaf still hangs on this tree as the new bud grows but the dead leaf will soon fall off. How could this picture help someone understand the idea of life after death?

One of the questions people try to make sense of is: 'What happens after you die?' On pages 18 and 19 we saw that the majority of the population thinks death is not the end. Most think there is some sort of spiritual dimension to existence but they don't know what.

Christians are sure there is life after death and the way we live will determine what happens next. It is perfectly logical, they say. All our behaviour has consequences, whether it is telling lies or causing **global warming**. Life on earth is not a brief, isolated event, it is a preparation for an eternal life. Christians believe God will judge us on the way we have behaved in life when deciding what happens next. Christians are confident there is life after death because that is what Jesus taught. His own **resurrection** is further evidence of this.

Activity

1 Draw a strip cartoon that shows someone doing something and the consequences of their action.

2 Do you think life after death has to be earned, or do people receive it automatically?

Jesus' resurrection

By allowing himself to be killed then buried, Jesus was able to overcome death. Three days later, Christians believe that God raised Jesus from the dead. This was to show people that death is not the end of existence for those who have faith in God.

Jesus said:

'For what my Father wants is that all who see the Son and believe in him should have eternal life. And I will raise them to life on the last day.'

(John 6:40)

3 **What does Jesus say is necessary for a person to be given eternal life?**

4 **Notice that Jesus still says a person must die first before they gain eternal life. Which words show this?**

5 a **Check the evidence for Jesus' resurrection. Choose *three* of the references listed below and explain who saw what.**
   - **Luke 24:13–35**
   - **John 20:1–18**
   - **John 20:19–29**
   - **John 21:1–14**
   - **1 Corinthians 15:5–7**

   b **Could any of these witnesses have been mistaken or bribed to say what they did?**

   c **Who do you think is the least reliable witness and who the most? Why?**

6 **What sort of evidence would you need to make you believe someone had returned from the dead?**

Heavens above!

Nobody knows what heaven is like because no one has come back to tell us about it. This hasn't stopped people speculating. Here are a few Christians talking about their ideas of life after death.

1 *I think that after you die, you go straight to heaven. What's it like? Well, it's just fantastic, everything will be perfect. You will be with people you love and no one will be sad.*

2 *When you die you get buried or burned, whatever you choose. It doesn't matter. Eventually – I don't know how long you have to wait, but you won't notice time – Jesus will appear and bring you back to life. I think you will get your body back but not with any diseases or old age, just in its best form. Then, you will be judged. Those who tried to do what God wanted will go to heaven and those who led a terrible life will be punished.*

3 *It is impossible to know what will happen after we die. We have only got a human brain, so we would never be able to get our head around such a difficult concept. But I'm sure that there is life after death. The Bible says there is. All religions believe in it and people have throughout history.*

4 *Heaven is just being with God. Hell? Well, I don't think it exists as a place. It's just not being with God. Anything else would seem terrible. There has to be a heaven and a hell as the ultimate reward or punishment for this life.*

7 a **Divide your sheet into four boxes and in each write the key points of each person's speech bubble.**

   b **What do the speakers agree on? What are the major differences in their views?**

   c **Draw a speech bubble and write your own ideas about what might happen after death.**

objective

to look at the use of art to convey a spiritual idea

glossary

Icon
Orthodox Church
Saint

The code breakers

1 Describe the person shown in picture **A** as fully as you can. Do you think you can make any guesses about his character, sense of humour and what he would be like as a friend? What is the evidence for your ideas?

People find it extremely difficult to imagine something other-worldly which is hardly surprising. Words frequently don't help and so people turn to more expressive art forms. Christians from the **Orthodox Church** use **icons** to help in their worship. The icon on your computer is just a tiny image that you click on to open up a much bigger picture. From there, you can probably move further into the programme, then the possibilities are endless.

Icons are similar for Christians. They sometimes call an icon 'a window into heaven' because the very simple image can open the way into deep thoughts which bring the worshipper closer to God.

Christians do not worship icons, even though an outsider might think they do when they see them kiss the image or put a lighted candle in front of it. It is the same as someone who has got a photograph of a person they love. They might gaze at it several times and it is quite clear the picture is very special to them. In fact, they would be really upset if you screwed it up and threw it on the ground. You know they are not devoted to the piece of paper. It's the real person they are thinking of. It is just the same with an icon.

2 a Use the 'Key to the code' (opposite) to read picture **B**. Then write a brief description of what the artist has done to show worshippers what life in heaven is like.

   b Do you think the icon in **B** conveys more information than a photograph would? Why?

Key to the code

- Large eyes, large ears and long nose show the saint is listening and thinking about God, and smelling the sweetness of heaven. Mouth and hands are small because the **saint** is so full of God's power s/he does not need to say or do much.

- Bright face shows the person is filled with the light of God.

- No strong light or shadows because everywhere is filled with the light of God.

- Halo around the head shows the Holy Spirit is at work.

- Colours have meaning and they are not necessarily intended to be life-like. Reddish brown stands for humanity. Red for the blood of martyrs. Blue for divinity. Warm colours show the joy and peace of heaven. Cold colours, the suffering and struggles on earth.

- Things get bigger in the background because we are looking through a window into heaven.

- Clothes have neat folds to show the calm harmony of heaven and white highlights reflect the spiritual world.

- Icon looks flat so artist can make important people and objects the size he wants.

- Figures sometimes go outside the frame to show they have no boundaries.

- Buildings may have strange perspectives to show that God sees the whole world at once.

Activity

3 What does the modern British icon painter, Brother Aidan, mean when he says icons are intended to 'introduce you to reality, not to imitate nature. It is to show you not what you see, but what is real.' (*Faith in Conservation*, 2003)

4 What other art forms could be used to help people understand ideas that are beyond words?

objective

to examine the different aspects of authority

glossary

Free will

Who says?

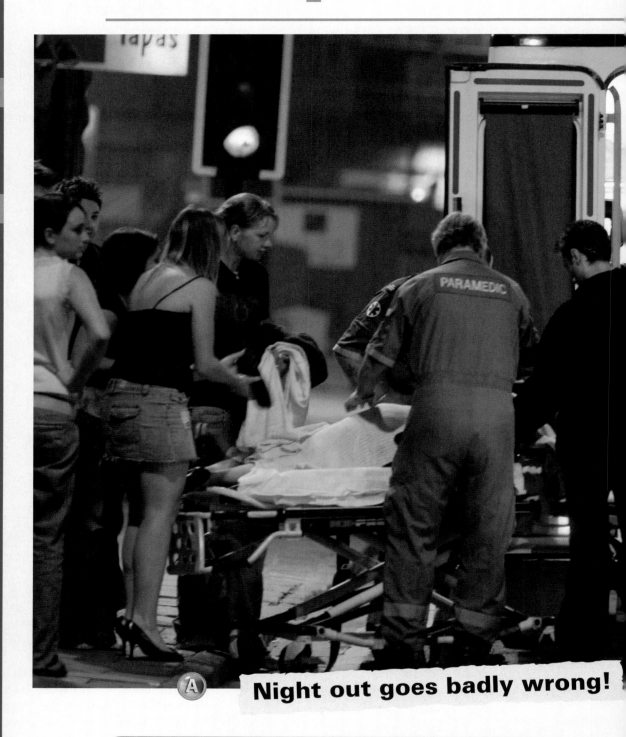

(A)

Night out goes badly wrong!

1 a Make up your own newspaper headline for picture **A**. Then add a report of around 150 words.

b We all know binge drinking is wrong. List as many possible reasons as you can that show it is wrong. Hint: Think about the effect this behaviour has on everyone involved.

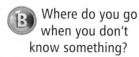

B Where do you go when you don't know something?

 Activity

2 a List *10* places or people you might turn to when you need to know something.

 b Against each, write a brief example of the type of thing they could help you with. For example, you would not go into the Post Office to ask where your socks were, and your Mum may not be the person to ask if you wanted a form to apply for a passport.

 c Draw a line from each item on your list to indicate where you get the information from. Is it possible to take it back further? Is there one source where everybody gets information from, or are there several places?

If you had to answer the following questions, where would you look for guidance?

1 Should I think about applying to university?
2 Is it likely to rain this afternoon?
3 Are woodpeckers in danger of becoming extinct?
4 How much of my birthday money should I save?
5 Is it wrong to walk by a charity collector without giving anything?
6 Should I tell my friend their hair looks a complete mess?

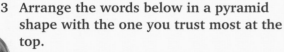 *Activity*

3 Arrange the words below in a pyramid shape with the one you trust most at the top.

Best friend. Parent. Teacher. Priest. Gut feeling. Librarian. Passer-by you chat to in the street. Worker in the Citizens' Advice Bureau. Internet.

Your conscience

Most people have a conscience which is our personal authority on what is right and what is wrong. That doesn't mean we take notice of it though. We may know the right thing to do, but choose to do something completely different and then feel guilty. What tells your conscience the answer? Strangely, there does seem to be agreement about what is right and what is wrong.

A Christian would say their conscience is the voice of God guiding them. Because we have been given **free will**, we don't have to take notice of that inner voice if we don't want to.

A Humanist would agree that everyone has a conscience. It is there to help you out with difficult personal questions. They say our conscience is simply a part of our character. The reason there is general agreement about what is right and wrong is because we are all humans and have similar instincts about the best way to get on with each other.

Activity

4 a A Christian would turn to God to help them decide. A Humanist would use their reasoning powers to decide what was right or wrong. What helps you decide how to act?

 b If you walk past some rubbish outside an empty shop and spot £5 in coins, what should you do? Would you behave differently if it was £50, £100 or £5,000? Why? How do you decide what to do in a situation like this?

C

27

objective

to understand why some people look to God as their source of authority and what that means for them

glossary

Covenant
Ten Commandments

Christians believe human beings are not perfect, everyone has weaknesses. The only perfect being is God, so Christians turn to God for guidance on how they should behave. For Christians, and all religious believers except Buddhists, God is the ultimate source of authority. There is nothing greater.

1 Look back to pages 12 and 13 and list the things Christians believe God can do. Against each point, write down the advantage this has over human abilities – remember humans only live for around 90 years maximum.

A What is the problem with letting everyone make up their own minds about what is right and what is wrong? Would you get total agreement?

B This painting shows the traditional idea of God as a terrifying figure of authority.

God the Father

Christians think of God as a father-figure. This involves a caring role as well as an authoritarian one. Think about the sort of authority a parent exercises in a family. It is worth comparing types of parents you have seen in films, TV programmes and books with your own experiences. Then consider how these different roles could be applied to a spiritual figure.

> **2** Weigh up the advantages and disadvantages of having a person in charge of an organisation. You might find it helpful to consider how a school would function without a head teacher, or without anyone in charge at all. Could it be left to pupils to decide what is right and what is wrong about a situation? Do you think people need rewards and punishments in order to make them behave?

There certainly can be advantages in having one person in charge who can help everyone else to know what they should be doing. If the authority is not human, but superhuman, then people need to discover how they can contact this being to understand what is required of them.

Some Christians believe that direct communication with God is the most reliable way of learning the truth. If you look back to pages 16 and 17 you will be able to remind yourself of ways Christians communicate with God. Others will look to books or people to pass the information across.

The authority of God

Christians believe God exerts his authority in various ways. One of these is through a set of 10 rules, known as the **Ten Commandments**, which were handed down hundreds of years ago. Those who argue that Christians should take them seriously point out that they are 10 commandments and not 10 suggestions as cartoon **C** jokes. It is worth remembering that when God gave the Ten Commandments to Moses and the Jews, they had to accept them in their entirety. The story in Exodus makes it clear that if the Jews wanted to accept the **covenant**, which was a special relationship with God, then they must accept it on God's terms. They could not pick and choose the parts they liked.

> **3 a** Read the Ten Commandments in Exodus 20:1–17.
>
> **b** What justification do you think God might give for each commandment being included?
>
> **c** If the Ten Commandments were first being given in the twenty-first century, what commandments do you think are important to include? Why?

I thought it was three strikes and you're out!

29

objective

to examine the
Bible as a source of
authority

glossary

Baptism

Let's have it in writing

What's so good about a book?

A book is useful because once
something is written down, it
is there forever. The content of
a particular book doesn't
change and the words are there
for all to read. They can be
consulted any time. Another
advantage of a book is that it
can be transported from place
to place – even to places where
there are no computers or
Internet access! Information
can be passed from person to
person through a book, even if
one of the writers has been
dead for hundreds of years.
Books can also hold more
information than a person, so
facts don't get forgotten or
muddled.

Can I have that in writing?

A Why are we so keen to get something
down in writing? Is the written word
more powerful than the spoken one?

1 Decide what the advantages and disadvantages would be if your
school was 'run by the book'. All decisions about behaviour,
uniform, discipline and activities would be made by looking in a
large rule book or database. Would it work?

All religions have their holy book. This is because the followers needed
something to refer to. It gives them rules for living. Although times
change and new technologies invent things no one could have
imagined, people don't change. Personal relationships and problems
remain the same. Because everyone is referring to the same book, it
unites them.

2 Write down *five* personal
problems which are unlikely to
have changed over time. Could a
book supply the answers to any
of them?

Rules and laws There are basic rules which were set out in ancient times to ensure people could live together peacefully. For example, don't steal and don't murder. There are also more specific rules given to the Jews about daily life, such as what food they should and shouldn't eat, how they should treat a debtor, what to do about a skin rash, etc.

Pieces of history These passages give accounts of the history of the Jews, what battles they fought, who their leaders were and such like.

Stories Some of these are totally fictional but have a meaning like the parable Jesus told about The Lost Son (Luke 15:11–32). Others are based on factual accounts of ancient heroes like David and Goliath or Daniel in the lion's den.

WHAT IS IN THE BIBLE?

Prophecies These passages predict the future.

Poetry Some of these are songs of praise to God, others are love songs.

An account of Jesus' life This recounts what Jesus did and taught.

Letters These were written to early Christians telling them how to lead the sort of life Jesus wanted.

Proverbs These are wise sayings, for example: 'A rich man has to use his money to save his life, but no one threatens a poor man'; 'A lie has a short life, but truth lives on forever'; or 'Watch out for people who grin and wink at you; they have thought of something evil'.

Why is the Bible special?

Christians think the Bible is special because it tells them exactly what God wants them to do. Some people refer to the Bible as 'the word of God' because they are convinced that the book was dictated to people by God. This gives it great authority.

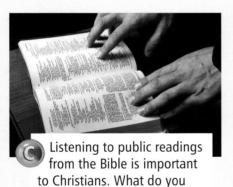

Listening to public readings from the Bible is important to Christians. What do you think they gain from it?

Other Christians think the words were composed by people who were inspired by God. The words are those of humans but this still makes the Bible more important than any other book. Christians feel they can trust what the Bible says and they will always be able to find something relevant to their daily life.

How do Christians use the Bible?

The Bible is used in different ways. Some Christians use it for private worship, reading a passage and using it as the basis for their prayers. When groups of Christians worship together, the priest might read passages aloud, or take one part and explain its meaning. Special passages are read at festivals and at celebrations like marriage or **baptism**. Smaller groups of Christians meet to read and discuss passages from the Bible believing that study will give them a better understanding of God's message.

3 The Bible provides Christians with a framework for living by telling them what is right and what is wrong. What do you base your ideas of right and wrong on?

Activity

to examine the
importance of the
life and teachings of
Jesus for Christians
today

glossary

Divine
New Testament
Old Testament
Revelation

Authority of Jesus

Who is Jesus?

Historically, Jesus was a Jew who lived in Israel around 2,000 years ago. Few details have been recorded about most of his life except for the last two years. Jesus was an important teacher and leader who attracted such a large following that both the Jewish authorities and the occupying Roman power were frightened. Although Jesus never intended to overthrow them with military power, the political authorities thought he meant trouble. Without any real evidence, Jesus was arrested, put through a sham trial then executed. This is a historical fact.

For Christians, Jesus is more than just a historical figure. They believe that three days after his death, God brought Jesus back to life to show people that there was everlasting life for those who believed in him. By giving his life for crimes he had not committed, Jesus paid for all the sins people had committed throughout history. In the future, people who believed in Jesus as the Son of God would be saved.

Christians understand that Jesus has two parts to his nature. The historical figure is the role model but Christians believe Jesus is also **divine**, since he was the Son of God. Although the human Jesus died nearly 2,000 years ago, Christians believe the divine Jesus is alive today in another dimension and can help them.

Ⓐ The artist Antonia Rolls said the inspiration for her unusual painting was that Jesus could well be sitting right next to you now. In the rush of our daily life, we don't stop to notice the person squashed next to us or even give them a second thought.

How can Jesus be a source of authority?

Christians believe that Jesus is the human face of God and the key to understanding what God wants us to do. Because Jesus actually lived the life of a human being, he showed people by example how they should behave. His teachings, and the answers he gave to people's questions, supplied information about God's will and gave meaning to life on earth.

Although Christians may differ in the way they interpret some of Jesus' words, they are united by their belief in Jesus as the Son of God. They all look to him for authority for what they do. They may do this by referring to the Bible which has prophecies about Jesus in the **Old Testament** or to his words and actions in the **New Testament**.

Christians are sure they can have a personal relationship with the divine Jesus through prayer. Some people also believe it is possible to receive a **revelation**, which is a sudden mystical experience of Jesus. This might be through a dream or an unexplained happening like the miracle described on pages 38 and 39.

Growing closer to God

Christians try to get closer to God by reading stories of Jesus' life in the Gospels. These form the basis of Christian worship and extracts are read at church services and special celebrations like baptisms and marriages, as well as at festival times. Parts of Jesus' life are re-enacted symbolically; this may be through nativity plays or as part of worship. Jesus' last supper on earth is regarded by Christians as having great spiritual significance and so parts are re-enacted regularly in the Holy Communion service in church.

Some of Jesus' words form the basis of hymns, prayers and sermons for Christians to think about in public or private worship.

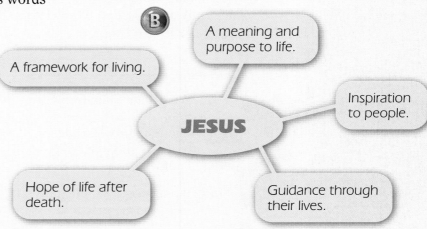

B

- A framework for living.
- A meaning and purpose to life.
- Inspiration to people.
- **JESUS**
- Hope of life after death.
- Guidance through their lives.

C Compare this traditional painting of Jesus with the one on page 32. Which do you prefer?

Activity

1 Copy the spider diagram in **B** and within each bubble write an example of how Christians gain these forms of support from Jesus' life or teachings.

2 Christians believe Jesus has the authority to show them the right way to lead their lives. Where does Jesus get his authority from?

3 Christians say they get strength from Jesus' example. Where do you get strength from?

objective

to look at different ways people can be sources of Christian authority

glossary

Martyrdom
Quaker

Personal authority

The public response to the death of Pope John Paul II was astounding. From all around the world Christians came to pay their last respects to this great Christian leader. It took some people 14 hours of queuing to reach the church where his body lay in state. Three to four million people are thought to have been in Rome for the funeral and millions more around the world watched extracts of this Christian leader's funeral on television. No celebrity, religious leader or member of a royal family anywhere in the world has ever been shown that sort of respect.

> **1 a** What *four* reasons might people give for joining the queue to pay their last respects to Pope John Paul II?
>
> **b** What might people gain from the experience?

A The queue that assembled in Rome to pay their last respects to Pope John Paul II in April 2005 was estimated to be five miles long at one point.

A spiritual leader

People often find it helps their faith to have a spiritual leader. They find it easier to identify with a real person than with an old book. You can ask a person a question and, if you don't understand the answer, ask it again in a slightly different way. A real live person who lives in the modern world can understand modern problems. They can react to issues and give a judgement on a situation and provide leadership for the whole group. There can be situations where someone does have to make a decision and lead from the front. Their example can be an inspiration to other Christians.

Traditionally, Christians have always had a leader. It began with Jesus, then passed on to St Peter and Roman Catholics believe the same direct line of leadership has passed on through the popes. Other Christian groups have their own leaders both at a national and local level.

> **2** What problems could there be if matters were decided by the person who became the leader each time, rather than by a book?
>
> **3** Design a job advertisement for the spiritual leader of a Christian organisation. What qualities would you look for in a person who will have authority over thousands of Christians? You will also need to bear in mind that they may have to present the religion to the media.

Unofficial spiritual leaders

Sometimes spiritual leaders appear accidentally. A person who never thought of themselves as a leader might find that others are inspired by their example.

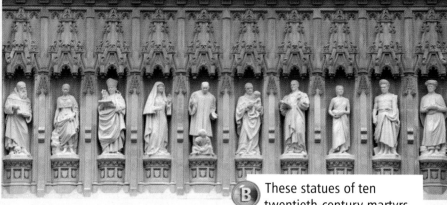

The front of Westminster Abbey contains ten modern statues of twentieth-century Christians who found themselves unofficial spiritual leaders. They were men and women who stood up for what they believed in and found the strength to hold on to their religious belief even though it cost them their life. In each case, their **martyrdom** made them into an unofficial spiritual leader.

People don't necessarily have to die to become leaders. The famous nun Mother Teresa found others looked to her for spiritual guidance as she cared for the poor and dying in India.

B These statues of ten twentieth-century martyrs are on the front of Westminster Abbey and were unveiled in 1998. The Christians represented are St Elizabeth of Russia, Manche Masemola, Esther John, Maximilian Kolbe, Lucian Tapiedi, Dietrich Bonhoeffer, Wang Zhiming, Janani Luwum, Oscar Romero and Martin Luther King.

Activity

4   Choose *one* of the twentieth-century martyrs to research further. You can find details about them on Westminster Abbey's website as well as in library books. Write a short piece for a Christian magazine that gives details of the person's work. Finish by explaining how Christians today might find inspiration from that person's life.

5   What sort of problems might someone have if people regard them as an unofficial spiritual leader?

Everyone is a leader

There are a few Christian groups who believe everyone is capable of religious insight and so there is no need for a spiritual leader. The **Quakers** do not have any priests. They call this 'the priesthood of all believers'. When they gather to worship, they sit in a circle around an ordinary coffee table, so everyone is equal. If anyone feels they want to share something personal or respond to a news item, or want to read a passage aloud, they will stand up and speak for a few moments, then sit down and let people quietly consider their words. Their remarks are likely to be thought-provoking and may well have spiritual implications.

Activity

6   Copy table **C** into your book and complete the advantages and disadvantages.

7   Choose *one* of the following Christians and find out how they became a spiritual leader. Give a short presentation to the class.

   ● St Paul (using Acts 9).
   ● Archbishop of Canterbury.
   ● Archbishop Desmond Tutu.

C

	Official leader	Unofficial leader	Everyone has a say
Advantages			
Disadvantages			

Yes, but is it true?

The proper name for a lie detector is a polygraph and, truthfully, it can't detect lies! What the machine can record are physical changes in a person. It might detect sweaty palms, an increased heartbeat, shakiness or rapid breathing. These symptoms can occur when someone is telling lies. But it is said that half the people who failed a lie detector test were actually telling the truth. They were just nervous!

> 1 Discuss with a partner whether or not it affects your enjoyment of a film if you know it is based on a true story. Why?

The plain simple truth

When somebody gives us some information, one of the first things we often ask is, 'Is it true?' Based on the answer, we will either listen without paying much attention then probably forget it, or listen carefully and decide what action to take. The truth matters a great deal to us.

When you are asked to 'tell the plain simple truth' it sounds easy, but, as one wit put it, 'The truth is never plain and rarely simple.' Think about the 'truthful statements' people give the police after they have witnessed a road accident. Their accounts can vary wildly, yet each person is convinced they are telling the truth. Why is this?

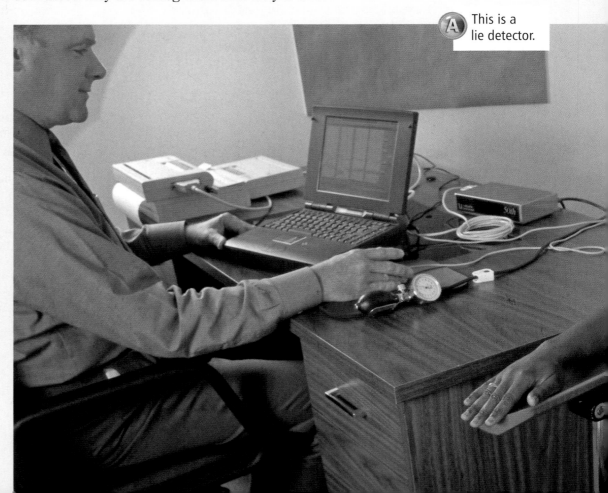

A This is a lie detector.

Scientific truth In science, when you want to discover a truth you conduct an experiment. One result isn't enough to prove it, is it? You have to conduct the same experiment many, many times. Only if the result continues to be the same, do you conclude that you have discovered a scientific truth. Strangely, this sort of truth is called a scientific theory and may not be true forever. A scientific theory is only true until someone proves it wrong in the future!

Legal truth To find out the truth in a court of law, 12 independent people listen to as much evidence as can be found. The whole group is asked to decide what is true 'beyond all reasonable doubt'. Once again, there is an acceptance that this is the best we can come up with as humans. A trial only takes place once to establish the truth.

TRUTH

Religious truth Christians believe that God can reveal the truth to people in different ways, in the Bible or directly through prayer or worship. Religious believers are convinced that God's truth is the whole truth because God has a greater power than humans. The differences arise when people have to pass the information on to others. They are only human and could make mistakes.

I just know it's true We often have a gut feeling about what is true and what is false. The feeling may be very strong and it can be hard to collect the evidence for this truth and impossible to prove. Deciding whether you are truly in love is one example. How do you test that?

Historical truth When people want to uncover the truth about the past they turn to old documents or archaeological evidence. How people interpret this evidence may vary.

B

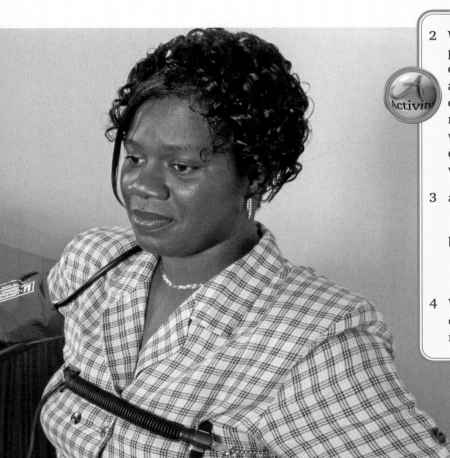

2 With a partner, discuss the sort of problems that might arise if the methods of discovering the truth were swapped around. For instance, would it work if courts of law adopted the scientific method of discovering the truth? They would hold the trial many times with different juries before accepting the verdict.

3 a Are there any other kinds of truth you would like to add to spider diagram **B**?

   b Which truth in the spider diagram do you think most people would be able to agree with?

4 Write the word 'Truth' in the centre of a double page and draw your own mind map.

Activity

Miracle or coincidence?

objective

to learn about the sort of things Christians consider to be miraculous and consider our own response to miracles

glossary

Coincidence
Miracle

Marvin Andrews, centre-half for Rangers, is said to be living proof that **miracles** can happen if someone puts their faith in God. In March 2005, Andrews seriously injured his knee playing for Rangers against Dundee. Medical experts agreed that the damaged ligament would require surgery followed by months of rest. Instead, Andrews turned to God for help. 'I respect the medical people at Rangers but I don't want to have the operation,' he said. 'I know it is hard for people to understand but God has given me strength. He is in control of my life and I believe it will be fine.' To the amazement of his team and the medical profession, Andrews carried on playing and had no pain. Doctors are unable to explain his recovery.

This is not Andrews' first experience of miracles. Seven years earlier when playing for Raith Rovers he suffered a pelvic injury. At the time, many feared his playing career was over but doctors insisted that if steel pins were inserted into his groin, he would be able to play again. Andrews was in such great pain that he considered giving up completely until a fellow team-mate introduced him to a Christian minister. The Pentecostal minister gave Andrews faith when he said nothing was impossible with God. 'I told him to go and play,' Pastor Joe said. 'He believed that God was going to help him and that was when a miracle happened. From there, his career took off.' Not only did Andrews recover but within a short time he also received an offer to play for Rangers.

(Quotes from 'Rangers centre-back whose game rests on divine intervention' *The Guardian*, 21 May 2005)

A

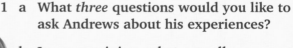

1 a **What *three* questions would you like to ask Andrews about his experiences?**

   b **In your opinion, what actually happened in Andrews' case? Could it be a miracle or is there another explanation for his recovery?**

2 **Discuss: Do miracles just happen to religious people? Could they happen to somebody who doesn't believe in God?**

Science and religion

How do you define a miracle?

It is worth thinking about the difference between a miracle and a magic trick. Most people would say they are very different. How would you define a miracle? One idea is that a miracle is an event that breaks the normal rules of nature.

Sometimes what one person calls a miracle, another doesn't. Read this:

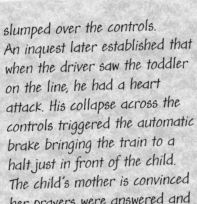

A little toddler escapes from his Mum and runs on to the railway track. As his panic-stricken mother races to reach him, she prays that God will save her son from the oncoming train. Suddenly the train pulls up only metres from the child. As his relieved mother grabs hold of him, she thanks God for answering her prayers with a miracle. When she looks up at the train she sees the driver slumped over the controls. An inquest later established that when the driver saw the toddler on the line, he had a heart attack. His collapse across the controls triggered the automatic brake bringing the train to a halt just in front of the child. The child's mother is convinced her prayers were answered and a miracle saved her son's life. What do you think? Why?

For Christians, the biggest miracle was Jesus' resurrection after being dead for three days. It is a miracle because no human, who has been dead for that long, has ever come to life again. Christians see this as evidence that God can intervene in human life.

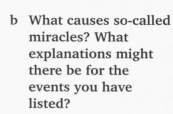

3 a List *four* things people might call miracles. Put a tick against any you would accept as miracles.

b What causes so-called miracles? What explanations might there be for the events you have listed?

4 a Make up a story where an event happens that some people call a **coincidence** and others a miracle.

b Do you think it matters if people have different views of the same event?

5

memo

FROM: Head of production
TO: Head of research

Because there is a lot of interest in miracles at the moment, we are planning a TV documentary for the autumn. Can the team work on it this week?

- We have got a one-hour slot between 8 and 9 pm on the last Wednesday in October. Programme needs to be in three parts to fit around the adverts.

- We've got to be even-handed – religious, scientific and non-believers. Any ideas about who we should interview?

- Draft a plan for each part of the programme. Make sure we leave the viewers to make up their own mind at the end.

objective

to consider the relationship between science and religion

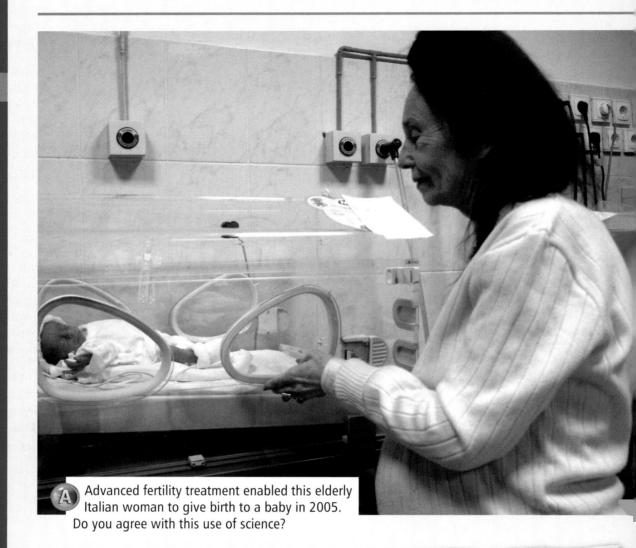

A Advanced fertility treatment enabled this elderly Italian woman to give birth to a baby in 2005. Do you agree with this use of science?

B

63-year-old gives birth to her first baby

63-year-old Mrs Subramaniam gave birth to a healthy baby boy in February 2004. She is the world's oldest first-time mother. Her little son, weighing 1.75 kilos, was delivered by caesarian section. Using the 74-year-old husband's sperm and an egg donated by the woman's niece, scientists developed a fertilised embryo in the laboratory for five days before implanting it in the mother's womb.

Activity

1 Role-play a radio phone-in between the scientists who performed Mrs Subramaniam's fertility treatment and members of the public. What sort of questions do you think people will be longing to ask?

2 Write a magazine article about Mrs Subramaniam's experience and include an interview with her.

3 How different would your life be if you were the child of Mr and Mrs Subramaniam? What difficulties might arise in the life of the Subramaniam boy as a result of his unusual beginnings?

Scientists can give a very accurate account of how this unusual fertility treatment was carried out. What science cannot do is to say whether the treatment was right or wrong.

Just because you can do it, does it make it right? Do you think a full brain transplant should be allowed if it could be done? If you have the scientific knowledge and technology to make a weapon of mass destruction, does that make it right?

It has been said that science and religion are not in conflict, they are simply two different approaches to life. Both are searching for the truth. Science tells us how something is done, the mechanics of it. Religion considers the meaning of it, why something happens. Although they come from different directions, they don't necessarily contradict each other and we often need both views to get the full picture.

In the same way, you could give a scientific and an artistic response to a painting. The scientific assessment will tell you about the structure of the canvas, the chemical analysis of the paint and possibly something about the perspective. The artistic response will deal with how the painter reacted to the subject. It might also pass comment on whether the picture is liked or disliked. What is certain is that the two responses will be very different. Neither will be wrong, nor make the other response worthless.

Scientist Arno Penzias says:

Science doesn't solve life's problems. It may provide descriptions but it doesn't provide meaning.

Many Christians believe that God created humans as intelligent life and so it is right for us to use our intellect in a scientific way. The learned scientist Dr John Polkinghorne, who was professor of mathematical physics at Cambridge for 25 years before becoming an Anglican minister, says, 'I think that science and religion are complementary descriptions of the very rich and varied world of our experience.' He says that if he put his hand up in the air someone might ask, 'What's going on?' One reason that could be given might be that Dr Polkinghorne is going to wave to somebody. A scientific reply would immediately launch into a description of how the muscles in the body worked to raise the arm. Neither answer would be wrong.

One Christian said he was quite sure a powerful God could have snapped his fingers and created a ready-made world if he had wanted. Instead, what happened was much cleverer. God created an evolving universe in which the creatures could make themselves. It might surprise you to know that the person with the idea of an evolving universe was actually a Victorian vicar (author of the children's book, *The Water Babies*) speaking soon after the publication of Darwin's theory.

Activity

4 If someone in your year group developed a life-threatening illness, what sort of questions would people ask? Would they all involve medical science?

5 If science and religion offer different ways of looking at the same thing, does this mean science will never be able to give the full answer to questions about what we are doing here?

Where do we come from?

Some Christians are called **Creationists** because they base their understanding of the beginning of human life on passage **A** in the Bible. For them, the Bible is the word of God which accurately states how events happened in history. Creationists argue that humans are so distinctive and superior to other animals they could never have evolved from apes. Instead, they say, humans were made by an intelligent designer – in other words God. No one has found a series of skeletons, like those in picture **B**, which prove apes gradually changed to humans. Indeed, apes still exist today.

Some Christians, and non-Christians, think **Darwin's** Theory of Evolution is the most likely explanation for the beginning of human life on earth. As picture **B** shows, the belief is that over thousands of years humans developed from apes. The scientific evidence to support this theory is that we share the same DNA profile as chimpanzees. In fact, we are 99% the same.

A 'So God created human beings, making them to be like himself. He created them male and female, blessed them, and said, "Have many children, so that your descendants will live all over the earth and bring it under their control."'

(Genesis 1:27–28)

Christians who accept Darwin's theory as the most likely explanation of the beginning of human life also have no difficulty accepting the biblical quotation in **A**. For them, the Bible is a sacred

B Some scientists believe this is the way humans came to be.

text, inspired by God but written down by humans who expressed things in their own way. Because the Bible contains stories, fables and poetry, as well as historical information, it was never meant to be a scientific textbook dictated by God. For Christians who accept the Darwin theory, the account in Genesis is a story that shows God was the creator of the universe.

Activity

1 You will have noticed Darwin's argument is called a 'Theory' of Evolution. What does the word 'theory' mean? Why isn't it is called a 'fact'?

2 Opponents of Darwin's theory say it does not explain everything. Where do we get a sense of humour, kindness, an appreciation of beauty and romantic love from? Animals don't have these characteristics. How can you answer this?

3 a Divide your page into two. On one side, outline the Creationist's argument and their evidence. On the other side, outline the Darwinist's argument and their evidence. Award marks out of 10 to each side for how good you think their argument is.

  b What are the weaknesses in each argument?

In 2004, the complete skeleton of a tiny human was found by archaeologists in a cave in Indonesia (**C**). Although only one metre tall, wear on the teeth and growth lines on the skull revealed this to be an adult female of a type never seen before. Because she was a tiny cave-dweller, scientists nicknamed her 'the hobbit'. Six more skeletons of this species officially named *homo floresiensis* have been discovered at the site. They lived 13,000 years ago. Scientific analysis of the brain cavity showed this was a previously unknown species and not a pygmy version of *homo sapiens* or a dwarf human. Although its brain was the same size as a chimpanzee's, it was far more advanced and able to make complex stone tools and fire, as evidence alongside the skeleton showed. Scientific tests show that we are not descended from these 'hobbits'; they were a separate species which died out.

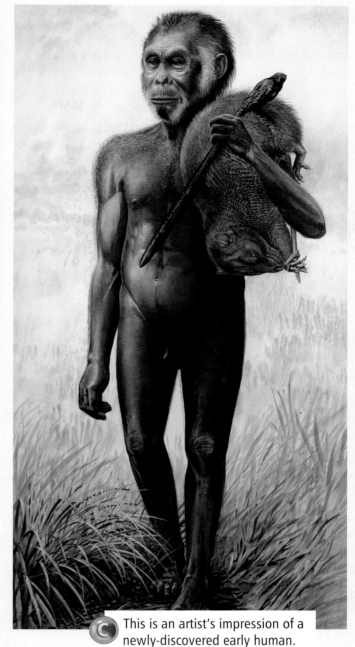

C This is an artist's impression of a newly-discovered early human.

Activity

4 Role-play a television debate between a Creationist and a Darwin supporter in the light of the 'hobbit' discovery. How could each use this new evidence to support their case?

5 Has the information from the 'hobbit' discovery changed your views about the origins of human life? Why?

Assessment for Unit 1

'One day Jesus got into a boat with his disciples and said to them, "Let us go across to the other side of the lake." So they started out. As they were sailing, Jesus fell asleep. Suddenly a strong wind blew down on the lake, and the boat began to fill with water, so that they were all in great danger. The disciples went to Jesus and woke him up, saying, "Master, Master! We are about to die!"

Jesus got up and gave an order to the wind and the stormy water; they died down, and there was a great calm. Then he said to the disciples, "Where is your faith?"

But they were amazed and afraid, and said to one another, "Who is this man? He gives orders to the winds and waves, and they obey him!"'

(Luke 8:22–25)

These questions test different sets of skills in RE. Which skills do you need to work on? Choose the level that you need and work through the tasks set.

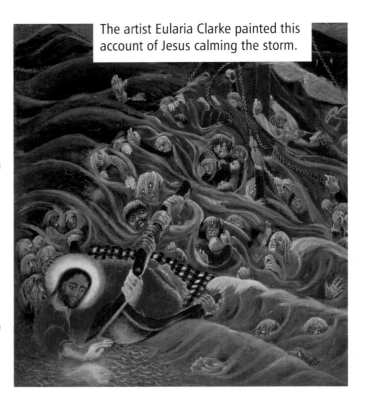

The artist Eularia Clarke painted this account of Jesus calming the storm.

Level 3

- Which part of the story is the artist showing? What is the evidence for this?
- Give *three* ways the artist shows the difference between Jesus' reaction to the storm and what everyone else does.
- Christians draw strength from their belief in Jesus. What do you draw strength from?

Level 4

- Describe *three* sources of authority a Christian could turn to if they wanted to know what was right or wrong.
- Choose another religion and give *three* sources of authority a believer could turn to.
- What *three* sources of authority would you turn to if you wanted to know something? Explain which you value most, and why.

Level 5

- Describe what Christians believe will happen after they die.
- How do their ideas differ from a Humanist's view of life after death? Are there any similarities between the two?
- Make up a question you would like to ask a Christian and another you would like to ask a Humanist. How do you think they might answer?

Level 6

- Suggest *two* reasons why a scientist might say God does not exist. Suggest *two* reasons why another scientist would have no difficulty being a Christian.
- Professor Fred Hoyle said that the chances of a planet 'happening' to have the right conditions for human life were as likely as a hurricane passing through a scrapyard and creating a jumbo jet. What reasons could he give for the existence of life on earth? How convincing do you find his hurricane argument? What would you say was the reason why we are here?

Who is responsible?

Baby found in towel in telephone box

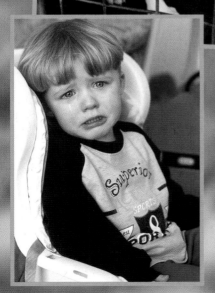

- List the problems that are shown on this page.

- Try to decide what might have caused the problems.

- Whose responsibility do you think it is to sort out the problems?

objective

to look at the way people decide what is right and what is wrong

glossary

Conscience
Humanist
Jesus

How do you know what's right and wrong?

A | Wrong | Depends | Right

Earlier in the book on pages 6 and 7 we considered questions that were hard to answer. Maybe there are some questions that can never be answered by humans but there will be times when we have to make a decision about what is right and what is wrong, no matter how difficult it is. Where do we look for answers?

Activity

1 a Copy the sentences shown in the statement bank on page 47 on to a sheet of paper then cut them out.

b Place them along a copy of the Right and Wrong scale (**A**) above. Place the ones you are uncertain about in the centre.

c Compare your results with a partner's.

● How much similarity was there in the outcome?

● How much agreement was there within the class?

● Where did the most differences and uncertainty arise?

● Was there any background information you would like to have known about any of the statements before you had to decide?

B When we do something wrong, we feel guilty. This is because we have got a conscience, but what tells our conscience an action is right or wrong? A religious person would say that it is God. If a person doesn't believe God exists, how do they decide what is right and wrong?

Statement bank

- You hide a class mate's schoolbag.
- You put glass bottles in the recycling bin.
- You lie to defend a friend from trouble.
- You give £1 to a street beggar.
- You tell a friend they look a mess.
- You hit someone who has been bullying your sister.
- You copy the maths homework from a friend.
- You flush an unwanted goldfish down the toilet.

You don't need a religion to tell right from wrong – any reasonable person can work it out for themselves, just by looking around.

Because **Humanists** do not think there is any evidence for God, they base all their decisions on reasoning power. They believe everyone has a **conscience**, which is a part of their mind and this warns them about the consequences of their actions. When we ignore our conscience it makes us feel uneasy, but when we act on its advice it makes us feel good. Humanists say our conscience is just part of our character and is developed by our upbringing.

C Zoe is a Humanist. Would you agree with her?

> **For Humanists there is one Golden Rule: Treat other people as you would like to be treated yourself.**

A religious person would look to God for guidance about what is right and what is wrong. Christians, like Humanists, would look to their conscience when deciding what is right and what is wrong about a situation. However, unlike Humanists, Christians believe that their conscience is guided by God. Many Christians would also agree that what they have learned from home, school and life plays some part.

You might recognise the Humanist's Golden Rule above. **Jesus** Christ simplified the many complicated rules that governed life in Jewish Palestine down to one for his followers:

'Do for others what you would want them to do for you.'

(Matthew 7:12)

The same rule appears in most religions. You could choose another religion and investigate what they say that is similar.

Activity

2 Write the Golden Rule in the centre of your page, box it with a coloured crayon. Then draw at least *six* lines from it. For each line, write down a crime that would disappear if everyone lived by the Golden Rule, for example murder.

3 Humanists say the Golden Rule is all you need. Can you think of any problems that might occur if this was the only law?

4 Other people say the things that help us to decide what's right and wrong are based on religion, upbringing and education. How would you rank these three in order of importance? Would you like to add any other influences to the list, such as friends?

objective

to think about lifestyle choices and their outcomes

glossary

Prayer

Jo Reynolds travelled the world working as a top model and rock musician. Here she talks about some of the choices she made.

I was brought up in a village in Berkshire. At secondary school I was hanging out with rebellious types and started shoplifting and bunking off lessons. It was the cool thing to do. I drank, went to raves and took Ecstasy, cocaine and acid. My parents tried to stop me, but I refused to be disciplined. I lied constantly about what I was doing and threatened to run away if anyone tried to control me...

At 18 I moved to London and started to hang around the cool nightclubs and shops – I wanted to get noticed and meet the right people. I had a shaved head and wore huge platform shoes, big false eyelashes and tiny miniskirts... I had to stand out in the crowd. My image became my selling point and my identity.

I started doing a bit of fashion modelling and was soon appearing in magazines.

I got a job at a nightclub, fell in with a gang and was soon on heroin.

My health started to fall apart. I had stomach problems, was violently sick and felt scared.

I continued to model, mostly for music videos... I started hanging out with a guy called Andrew, who taught me how to play guitar and write songs. We formed a band called Windscale. When Andrew and I broke up, so did the band.

I became depressed, and after all the years of having fun and getting away with it, now each time I took drugs I felt darkness coming into me. I started to get paranoid.

Things got worse and worse as Jo lost her grip on life and she had to rely on valium to calm her down.

I tried various things to get better – acupuncture, tarot cards, crystal healing and special diets. I became addicted to seeing psychics and fortune-tellers.

Then she met Stuart who asked her to join his band.

He was clean-living, fantastically talented and a really good and honest person. I completely fell in love with him. We toured America played in some amazing venues. It was very romantic.

Jo went on to do modelling for a fashion company owned by Prada, then for Italian Vogue and her modelling career really took off. When her relationship with Stuart fell apart, Jo became very depressed. She felt she couldn't cope and began eating as a comfort. That caused problems with modelling and the battle to stay thin led to anorexia.

Seeing what a state I was in, my friend Donna suggested I go on an Alpha course – an introduction to Christianity – and a food addiction programme… That night I went to church with Donna. I didn't understand any of the sermon, but I felt lifted up by the atmosphere and the music… I went to the front afterwards for **prayer** and a woman asked if I'd like to ask Jesus to come into my life and help me. Thinking, 'Well, I've tried everything else,' I said yes.

Several months later Jo decided to join the Alpha introductory course to Christianity but admits that she couldn't concentrate and didn't take much in. The people in the group were nice and she felt comfortable with them, so she carried on going.

…I sensed God was saying to me; 'You are whole.' And I knew I didn't need to go to my food addiction meetings any more. I was ready to let go. I still go through difficult times and I'm uncovering aspects of my life and my past that need dealing with. But instead of turning to people and to a programme to help me, I'm letting God heal me. It has been an incredible, strengthening process, but it's also been quite painful and tiring at times…

It was during the Alpha course that I really found my faith. It gave me the link into the church community that I needed to feel safe enough to trust God with my life.

Over the years I've done a lot of things I am really ashamed of, but now I know that I am forgiven. God has given me a second chance.

(Adapted from *Alpha News* 'The War Cry' 19 February 2005)

1   Draw a line down the centre of your page. On one side, list *four* different choices Jo made about the way she would lead her life. On the other side, write the outcome of each decision. What do you think was the turning-point for Jo?

2   Look through a magazine, or watch the adverts on an evening's television. List *six* things advertisers tell us make a good lifestyle. Would you agree with them?

3   What *four* things do you think make for a satisfying life? How important do you rank money?

4   Jo's story has been reprinted from the Christian magazine *Alpha News*. Why do you think the Alpha course organisers wanted people to read Jo's story?

5   Do you admire Jo or think she was foolish? What *three* questions would you like to ask Jo?

Can you live with yourself?

Humans are a higher order than all other animals. We have a conscience which is something that sets us apart from animals. That is one of the things that makes us human. You might think your dog has a conscience when you come in and he is looking guilty. Further inspection reveals that he has managed to open a kitchen cupboard and has scoffed a packet of breakfast cereal. Scientists would say that the dog's look is not the result of a guilty conscience but fear of the consequences. He doesn't think his action is morally wrong but he can remember from past experiences how you will react!

Humans are different. People generally feel guilty if they do something they know is wrong even when they aren't found out. Most Christians would say that this feeling of guilt is because of our conscience, which is guided by God.

1 In the USA most children are told the story of how George Washington, the first US president, vandalised a cherry tree with an axe. No one saw him do it but when his father saw the tree stump, he was furious and wanted to know who had done it. George Washington immediately owned up.

a Why do you think Americans are so proud of this story about their first president?

b Do you think their opinion of George Washington would have been different if it came out that he had lied?

c Would George Washington have been a better person if he hadn't chopped down the tree in the first place? Explain your view.

Self-respect

This often plays a greater part in the way we act than we realise. No one likes to think that they are a totally worthless person. Personal integrity does matter to us and can be the underlying reason why we do a good action even if no one knows about it. On the other hand, it is not just the fear of being caught out that makes us do the right thing. Most people have an in-built wish to do the right thing. This makes us different from animals.

Christians would say that it does matter how we treat each other. Even if another person doesn't know what you did or what your motive was, God does. Christians believe God knows everything we are thinking and doing, so no one can pretend to him. At the end of our life, Christians are sure we will be judged on all the things we did and thought.

It doesn't matter that I lied to him, he'll never find out.

B Would you agree? If no one knows what you did wrong, does that make it right? Why?

Activity

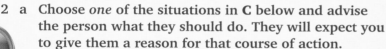

2 a Choose *one* of the situations in **C** below and advise the person what they should do. They will expect you to give them a reason for that course of action.

 b Do you think being a Christian might affect a person's response to the situations? Why?

C

- I am sure my close friend Vikki is doing drugs. She gets a bit cagey when I ask her about some things and she never used to be like that. It will totally wreck her plans to be a freelance artist and that's a pity because she is really talented. I get on well with her Mum, do you think I should mention my fears to her, or not? I don't think Vikki will listen to me.

- When our classroom was empty one day last week, I went in to get my kit for games. I noticed £10 on the floor near the back notice-board and pocketed it. It was mentioned later in the day that someone from another class had lost some money but I kept quiet. It might not have been theirs anyway. Should I own up now or not?

- Someone in our group thought she was pregnant and confided in me. She probably told some of the others too. Anyway, she said I mustn't tell anyone else but it was such a good bit of gossip I couldn't help myself. Kerry was upset later in the week when she heard people talking about her. She asked me if I'd told but I said no and she believed me. Anyway, she wasn't pregnant after all but I feel guilty. What should I do?

- I know there is bullying going on in our year but I don't want to say anything. I was bullied last year and I really hated it but if I say anything they'll turn on me again. I can't do anything, can I?

objective

to examine the rights and responsibilities of members of a modern family

glossary

Kibbutz

Happy families

1 List *four* things you think make for a happy family in the twenty-first century.

2 List *four* things that could threaten a modern family's happiness.

Your surname matters

It is no accident that we all have a surname, or a family name. The name of our family defines who we are. People often make snap judgements about someone they have just heard about based on their surname. 'Oh they are a nice family,' your Mum might say when you tell her about a new person in your class. It works the other way too and some people have a lot to overcome because they belong to a family that has got a 'bad name' for being in trouble with the law.

We tend to take the family structure for granted but there have been experiments in the past to improve on it. Some settlers in Israel in the middle of the twentieth century lived in a small village unit called a **kibbutz**. Because there was a lot of work to be done establishing these communities, couples were encouraged to have children then return to work. The baby moved into the baby-house along with all the other children and was looked

3 a Draw a spider diagram with the word 'Family' in the centre. The legs list all the advantages people might get from being part of a family. Think about practical things such as somewhere to live, emotional things such as having a sense of identity, and social things such as being taught how to behave towards others.

b Compare your results with the class and add any new ideas to your diagram.

after by professional childminders. The parents could visit their child whenever they liked, but the child had its meals and slept in the house with the other children. After many years, it was decided that this communal child-rearing wasn't working and families went back to looking after their own children.

4   What do you think the children missed out on when they were reared with other children in the kibbutz? Would the parents have missed out on anything?

5   The kibbutz originally believed there were advantages in children being brought up together. What might these have been?

Family rights and responsibilities

Only when you are a baby do you get all the advantages of being in a family without any of the responsibilities! Think about the members of your family and who exactly has responsibilities for things. (This is personal information and not for reading out.) When you think about it, responsibilities are wide-ranging and include things like locking up at night, looking after any animals, making sure the bills are paid, washing up, fetching the dustbin in, checking elderly relatives are okay, etc.

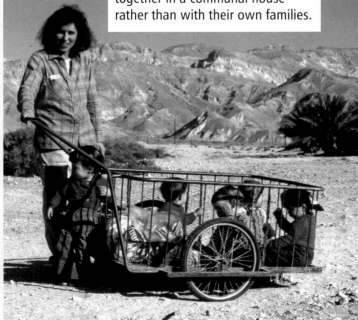

B This photograph was taken in Israel. All the children in this community, called a kibbutz, live together in a communal house rather than with their own families.

Trust

Trust is one of the important things in a family. Family life wouldn't work without it. Each of us trusts that another member of the family will do their bit. It's when they forget, or deliberately refuse to do so, that tempers get frayed.

Education in the family

Although everyone goes to school, we learn a great deal from our families. Many people would say we learn more from them than we ever do at school. Certainly, we are likely to remember the things we learned at home better because not only are we told it, but parents often put things into practice themselves. This goes for bad things as well as good!

6   Make a list of the things which members of your family assume, or expect, that you will do. This is private and not for reading out unless you want to.

> My Mum expects me to go to Tesco with her on a Friday night. I have got enough to do without having to push a trolley around. I don't think it's fair that she should expect me to battle round the supermarket every week. What can I say to her to get out of it?
> Sam

7   Reply to this 14-year-old's letter above giving advice and reasons.

8   What sort of things do you think families should be responsible for teaching their children? Is sex education one of them?

9   If a child does something wrong in the community, like spraying graffiti on a wall, is it the parents' responsibility? If not, whose responsibility is it?

Responsibility in a Christian family

objective

to understand how and why Christians place great emphasis on family life

glossary

Disciples
New Testament

Family life is an important part of Christian life. From scant details of Jesus' early life, it is clear that he was brought up in a caring family. Even when he was dying on the cross, he was concerned about his mother's welfare and asked one of the **disciples** to take care of her. Jesus' teachings also showed his followers how much he valued family life. In the parable of The Lost Son (Luke 15:11–32), Jesus gave an example of how a Christian father should behave towards his children.

Later in the **New Testament**, St Paul wrote letters to new Christian groups that were forming to give them advice on all aspects of the Christian lifestyle. In his letter to the Christians in Ephesus, he wrote about family responsibilities. It is interesting to notice that he told them that responsibilities worked both ways.

'Children, it is your Christian duty to obey your parents, for this is the right thing to do. "Respect your father and mother" is the first commandment that has a promise added: "so that all may go well with you, and you may live a long time in the land." Parents, do not treat your children in such a way as to make them angry. Instead, bring them up with Christian discipline and instruction.'

(Ephesians 6:1–4)

A Christians believe that family life is important. It is stressed in the marriage ceremony and couples are encouraged to have children and bring them up in the Christian faith.

As Christians, we believe family life is important and put a lot of effort into it. When the children were small we took them to the Family service at our church once a month. Now they are older we attend morning service together as a family most Sundays. Sarah has chosen to go to a Christian youth club and Jake is learning to be a bell-ringer at our church.

Ethics and relationships

54

1 What is the idea behind this saying from the book of Proverbs below? Make up a short story that shows this idea in action.

'Discipline your children while they are young enough to learn. If you don't, you are helping them to destroy themselves.'

(Proverbs 19:18)

2 Produce an A5 leaflet Christian parents could be given when they ask the priest about having their baby baptised. Explain what the Christian attitude towards family life is. You will need to research the baptism service to find out what promises the parents make to God about the upbringing of their child.

3 a Christians believe responsibility is a two-way thing. Make a list of the responsibilities that a parent has to their child, and another to show the responsibilities that the child has to a parent.

   b Are there any situations where you think these responsibilities no longer apply?

4 Role-play a scene between a Christian parent and their teenage son or daughter. The parent wants the teenager to attend a Christian youth camp in the holidays and the teenager doesn't want to go.

I have started to go to Holy Disorder which is a great way of meeting other young Christians. It's not exactly a youth club because we plan our own worship as well as entertainment. I think it's great fun because we are all of a similar age with similar interests. As a Christian, I believe family life is important. I do try to be considerate towards other members of the family. Even though I am not keen on visiting all the relatives, I do try and go along with it. After all we are all family.

Both our children were baptised as babies and we take the promises we made to bring them up as Christians very seriously. When they were little, I read Bible stories to them and explained what they meant. Today, we often chat through problems that face them. I have to admit that I sometimes ask them for advice about issues too!

No, of course I don't agree with everything my parents say. I am only human! But I know that as a Christian I should treat them with respect and not bad-mouth them behind their back, or answer back.

Do you care?

objective

to review the idea that relationships mean responsibilities

glossary

Cohabiting

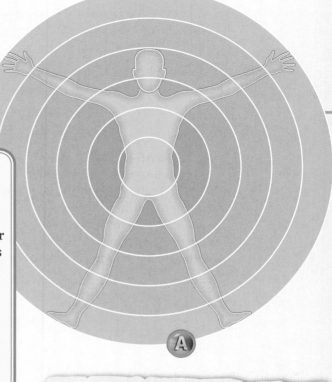

A

No one is completely on their own. We come into contact with lots of different people in our everyday life.

1 a Draw a copy of picture **A** in your book and write down the names or jobs of people you come into contact with on a regular basis, putting those closest to you on the inside. Include family, close friends, relations, people at school, those in any clubs or shops you go to regularly, etc.

   b Now think about what responsibilities, if any, you have towards each of the people in your diagram?

2 With a partner, consider what responsibilities, if any, you might have towards someone you hardly know. Is there a basic human responsibility towards a fellow human being? If someone collapses in the road outside the school, do you have a responsibility to do anything?

Activity

No one helped victim of mugging

Shoppers hurried past Shelley Thornton yesterday as she struggled with her attacker. As 17-year-old Shelley walked out of a chemist, she was punched in the face by a man who tried to snatch her handbag. She fought back but no one came to her aid. 'I kept praying that somebody would help me,' she said. 'But people just ignored me and hurried past.'

B

Why do you think nobody helped Shelley?

Close relationships

Relationships involve responsibilities on both sides. Perhaps that is why they can be intensely rewarding but equally, when they go wrong, they involve lots of unhappiness.

Members of religions also believe relationships matter. This is because their leaders and scriptures teach that God wants humans to treat each other well. After death, most believe they will be judged on the way they have treated other people. Many religions go further and set out the best type of relationships for people to follow.

Although members of the British Humanists Association do not believe in a god, they are convinced that personal relationships are very important. They say evidence shows that people who actively care about others form better relationships and have more rewarding lives.

C Do you think the media show us an unrealistic view of relationships? What examples could you mention to support your view?

Before we knew it we were having Häagen~Dazs.

Fall deeply in Häagen~Dazs.

Activity

3 a Devise a questionnaire to ask people in your year group what *five* qualities they would value most in a partner for life.

   b Plot your results on a graph. Compare your results with others in the class. What *three* qualities have come out top? How does this compare with the way relationships are depicted in soaps or in adverts?

4 List *four* points you think would make a dream relationship for you and then *four* points that could turn the same relationship into a nightmare.

A close relationship gives each partner the support and backing of the other. Clearly, many people think marriage has something that **cohabiting** (living together) doesn't because not only do they choose to marry but some will remarry even though their first marriage failed. What do you think they are gaining from a married relationship?

Forgiveness

Because none of us is perfect, things do go wrong in any relationship. Many people would say that one important ingredient in a lasting relationship is being prepared to forgive your partner. Equally, being able to say sorry when you have made a mistake is important.

Activity

5 Draw a mind map. Put the words 'Relationships bring responsibilities' in the centre of your page. Jot down all the ideas that come into your head connected with this. Draw links connecting the thoughts. Weigh up the advantages and disadvantages of being in a long-term relationship.

6 a Think of *three* situations where one partner may require forgiveness from the other. These need to range from a minor problem to a major one.

   b What would you recommend the couple did in each case? Why?

7 Look at the speech bubbles in **D** and decide how important you think it is to forgive your partner, and why.

D

It is a sign of weakness having to say you're sorry. I think it is important not to lose face.

I'd rather say sorry than risk us breaking up. We've got so much to lose.

Christian responsibilities in marriage

A Why do people choose to get married?

Jesus' teaching about marriage

'Haven't you read the scripture that says that in the beginning the Creator made people male and female? And God said, "For this reason a man will leave his father and mother and unite with his wife, and the two will become one." So they are no longer two, but one. No human being must separate, then, what God has joined together.'

(Matthew 19:4–6)

The Church of England says:

- Christians believe that marriage is a gift from God. In the marriage ceremony, a couple make a public declaration of lifelong commitment to love each other, come what may.
- The Bible compares married love with the love Jesus has for his followers. He expressed his love by being prepared to sacrifice himself, even to die for the people he loved. This is amazing and **unconditional love**. Jesus never said, 'I love you, but…' In our marriages we can try to follow his model by loving our partners in a self-sacrificial way, putting their needs before our own.
- Christians believe that marriage offers the right place for the fulfilment of our sexuality and that it provides a stable and secure environment for bringing up children.

Extract from a Christian marriage service

The priest, who takes the service, asks both the groom and bride in turn the following questions. These are the ones the priest asks the bride:

> [Name] will you take [Name] to be your husband? Will you love him, comfort him, honour and protect him, and, forsaking all others, be faithful to him as long as you both shall live?

Activity

1 List the things that this bride above is promising. Against each point, write an example of what each promise might involve.

2 Look back to pages 52–57 and the work that you did on relationships. Are there any other responsibilities you would like to add, or change, if you were planning a marriage service?

The congregation in the church are also expected to play their part and take the following vows.

> Will you, the families and friends of [Name] and [Name], support and uphold them in their marriage now and in the years to come?

3 What are the congregation promising to do? Is it fair to expect family and friends to be involved in someone else's marriage? Could they be of any help?

 How important do you think it is to have an outward sign of marriage?

The Church of England also says:

- Marriage is a gift of God in creation through which husband and wife may know the grace of God. It is given that as man and woman grow together in love and trust, they shall be united with one another in heart, body and mind as Christ is united with his bride, the Church.
- The gift of marriage brings husband and wife together in the delight and tenderness of sexual union and joyful commitment to the end of their lives. It is given as the foundation of family life in which children are born and nurtured and in which each member of the family, in good times and in bad, may find strength, companionship and comfort, and grow to maturity in love.

4 Fold a sheet of A4 paper to create a leaflet. Use the Church of England's information to design a leaflet that could be given to a couple choosing whether to have a church wedding or a civil one in a hotel. You need to tell them what Christian marriage means and what sort of responsibilities they would be agreeing to.

5 a Draw a table to compare what is said in a Christian wedding ceremony with a civil one.

b Which ceremony would you feel most comfortable with? Why?

c Some people choose to add extra promises to their civil ceremony. Are there any extra statements or promises you would add?

6 a What does the Church say are the advantages of living in a Christian married relationship?

b Do you think any of these points would be missing if a couple chose to have a civil wedding in a hotel?

c Would a relationship be any different if the couple chose to live together and never married?

The two statements in **C** are the only ones a couple has to make in a **civil wedding**. You will notice nobody makes any promises. Is this a more realistic start to married life?

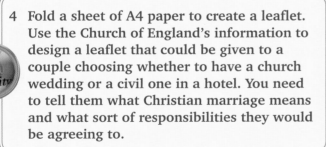

> I do solemnly declare that I know not of any lawful impediment why I [Name] may not be joined in matrimony to [Name].

> I do call upon these persons here present to witness that I [Name] do take you [Name] to be my lawful wedded wife/husband.

59

What are friends for?

You can choose your friends but you can't choose your relations

Obviously that is true and it has an impact on the way we treat our friends. Friendship is highly prized. As humans, we need other people's company. It makes us feel wanted, gives us a sense of belonging and helps our self-confidence. No matter how much we know, we still learn from friends and they learn from us. It is a two-way relationship.

Not only do we choose our friends, but they choose us and they can break off a friendship at any time. In a friendship there are special rules. Some things are totally wrong, yet they are not illegal. Breaking a promise is one of them. Can you think of anything else which is wrong in a friendship?

A Having friends makes all the difference to a person's life.

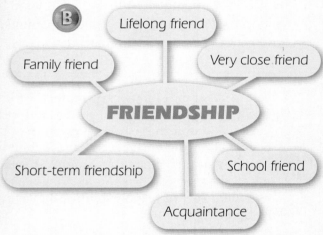

B

Lifelong friend

Family friend

Very close friend

FRIENDSHIP

Short-term friendship

School friend

Acquaintance

Activity

1 Draw a copy of spider diagram **B** in your book and add other sorts of friends that some people might have. Under each, add a few words to define that sort of friendship.

2 Make a list of *10* things you think you owe to your closest friend. These might include always being honest with them, backing them up when they are in trouble or possibly remembering their birthday.

3 Which are the *three* most important qualities in a friendship for you?

4 Write a helpful reply to *one* of the letters in **C** above. Explain what the person should do and why that is the right thing to do in the circumstances.

Christianity and friendship

Jesus never taught specifically about friendship but his actions showed Christians how they should behave towards their friends. **Gospel** stories show that Jesus had 12 close friends and, of those, Peter was the person he shared most things with.

As friends do, Jesus regularly ate and travelled to places with them.

Towards the end of his life when Jesus knew that he would be captured and crucified, he also knew that none of his friends would help him. 'This very night all of you will run away and leave me,' he told them. Peter was clearly upset his friend should think that of him. 'I will never leave you, even though all the rest do!' he said. But Jesus told Peter that not only would he escape, but when someone asked him about Jesus, he would deny ever knowing him.

D This painting is called 'The Betrayal'. It shows the moment when Judas, one of Jesus' close friends, gives Jesus away to the Roman Soldiers. See Matthew 26:47–50.

When soldiers did turn up to arrest Jesus all his friends ran off in fright. Peter did hang around outside the house where Jesus was imprisoned. Someone spotted Peter and said, 'You, too, were with Jesus of Galilee.'

'I don't know what you are talking about,' he said and quickly left.

When another person identified him, he got agitated and said, 'I swear that I don't know that man!'

Then someone else identified him, 'Of course you are one of them. I can tell by your accent!'

Peter hotly denied it, 'I swear that I am telling the truth! May God punish me if I am not! I don't know that man!'

As he walked away, Peter heard a cockerel crowing, then he remembered exactly what Jesus had said to him. 'Before the cock crows you will say three times that you don't know me.' Peter went out and wept bitterly.

(Taken from Matthew 26:69–74)

5 Should Peter have admitted he knew Jesus? If he had done, he would have been arrested, tried and executed. As it turned out, Peter was able to carry on Jesus' work and set up the Christian Church. But, on the other hand, he let his closest friend down. Jesus was prepared to die for Peter, but Peter lied to save his skin. Write a paragraph explaining what you think was the right course of action.

objective

to examine what leads some people to give their life for others

glossary

Mass
Resurrection
Saint

Would you give up your life for someone?

Jesus said:

'My commandment is this: love one another, just as I love you. The greatest love a person can have for his friends is to give his life for them.' (John 15:12–13)

The example of Jesus

Whilst many people have great affection for their friends, they may wonder at Jesus' command. Jesus did more than just say it. He put his teaching into practice. When God required his son to die at the age of 33 so that the rest of humanity could be given eternal life, Jesus accepted. It must be terrifying to know your future involves torture then an agonisingly slow death, but Jesus was prepared to do it to save others. His example has inspired many Christians to give their lives to save others. Below are stories of two well-known Christians but there have been plenty of less-publicised examples of people following Jesus' examples.

A Jesus was prepared to sacrifice his life for others. This has inspired some Christians to give their lives for others.

War produces great suffering but also great heroism. One Polish priest, Maximilian Kolbe, was arrested by the Nazis and taken to the death camp at Auschwitz. Despite being held in the most appalling conditions of starvation and brutality, Kolbe helped other prisoners. He gave no thought to his own suffering; instead he shared his meagre food rations, consoled people, organised secret prayer meetings and did everything he could to keep people's spirits up. Eventually, the Nazis could stand it no longer and executed him. People who saw his example and survived (and that included prison guards) told his story afterwards.

One bishop said later, 'The life and death of this one man alone can be proof and witness of the fact that the love of God can overcome the greatest hatred, the greatest injustice, even death itself.' In 1982, Maximilian Kolbe was made a **saint**.

Another Roman Catholic priest also took courage from the example of Jesus' death and **resurrection**. Oscar Romero publicly denounced the government death squads who roamed the countryside in El Salvador, killing at random. Romero knew the risks. His radio broadcasts condemning the government were dangerous and likely to cost him his life. But he said if his death helped bring justice, it would be worth it. When he received death threats his response was, 'Let my blood be a seed of freedom, and a sign that hope will soon be a reality.' He was taking **mass** in a hospital chapel when a single bullet fired through the window killed him.

His death was not wasted. International outrage at his assassination helped to bring about change and save lives, as well as inspire other Christians. Someone prepared to give their life for others, because Jesus did, is a very powerful example.

1 Do you think people who are prepared to lay down their life in war are putting Jesus' teachings into practice? Why?

2 In your opinion, was either Kolbe or Romero's sacrifice worth it? Why?

B Buying a poppy is one way British people show their gratitude for the sacrifices made in war.

Unsung heroes

There have been many less-publicised examples of people being prepared to give their life for others. Not all have been Christian, yet they have been prepared to make the ultimate sacrifice.

Jemma was pregnant with her first child when she discovered she had cancer. She was given the choice of having strong anti-cancer drugs but knew these would harm, probably even destroy, her unborn child. Instead, she chose to go through with her pregnancy without cancer treatment in order to give her child the chance of life. She knew that she would die as a result.

When Paul's brother had kidney failure, there was no question in Paul's mind but that he would donate one of his own kidneys no matter whether his health suffered. Fortunately, it didn't and both brothers have gone on to lead healthy lives.

3 With a partner, consider the similarities and differences between someone who dies in war and one of the examples opposite. Could you say one is 'better' than the other, or is it not that sort of thing?

4 As a class, discuss whether you think a parent should always be prepared to sacrifice their life for their child.

There have been numerous examples of people in sudden emergencies, who have thrown themselves over another person to shield them from harm. There are stories of other people going back into a burning building to try and rescue more people. In the process, they have given their life to save others.

Responsibility for strangers

'I was hungry and you fed me, thirsty and you gave me a drink; I was a stranger and you received me in your homes,… I tell you, whenever you did this for one of the least important of these members of my family, you did it for me!'

(Matthew 25:35 and 40)

Activity

1 a Read The Parable of The Good Samaritan in Luke 10:25–37.

   b What connection is there between this story and the quotation from Matthew above?

   c Write a short piece explaining what these two passages teach Christians about the way they should behave towards strangers and the reasons given.

There were also many instances when Jesus helped people whom he did not know. Most of the stories about people healed by Jesus concern strangers who approached him for help. In all cases, Jesus gave them the help they needed even though he had never met them before – and only a few returned to thank him!

A

THE **SALVATION ARMY** explain what happened to Janet: Janet had been abused by her father since she was 11. After a particularly horrendous assault, she fled to the city and began looking for work and somewhere to live. She fell straight into a vicious circle of homelessness – where someone cannot secure a job because they have no address, but they cannot afford somewhere to live until they have a job. Janet was torn between hardship and despair. Should she choose the isolation of life on the streets or the constant abuse of her father? In the end, it seemed the street was the lesser of two evils. Through the '**Soup Run**' we found Janet a place in a Salvation Army Centre for homeless women. After a few weeks, she successfully applied for a job in a hotel and later was able to rent a small flat of her own. We still see Janet when we pass the hotel on our nightly 'run'. Janet's is one of the few stories with a happy ending.

Christians understand that they should follow the example set by Jesus. Some groups have organised themselves to help strangers in need. Article **A** is a case study from the Salvation Army who run what they call an Outreach Team in London. There are hundreds (the exact number is not known) of people, young and old, who live on the streets of the capital. Some people categorise the homeless as either 'runaways', 'throwaways' or 'growaways'. 'Runaways' are people who have left home because of problems. 'Throwaways' are people who find themselves thrown out of the place they have lived in for some time and have nowhere else to go. It might be an institution like a children's home, prison, a mental hospital or even the army. 'Growaways' are a smaller group of young people who leave home believing they can start a new life on their own, but when it all goes wrong they have nowhere to turn.

B How could a policeman who was also a Christian minister be especially useful at the scene of a road accident?

2 Imagine your school held a fundraising event to help the homeless and raised £530. Below is a list of how the Salvation Army could put donations to good use. Read through it and decide how you would like to spend the £530 and give your reasons.

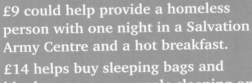

£9 could help provide a homeless person with one night in a Salvation Army Centre and a hot breakfast.

£14 helps buy sleeping bags and blankets to warm people sleeping on the streets.

£25 could pay for a 'Soup Run' serving on average 60 people a night.

£50 helps heat the Salvation Army Day Centre for one week.

£250 keeps a Salvation Army Drop-in Centre open throughout Christmas week.

3 Write an article for a police magazine that explains how satisfying a job it can be to become a police **chaplain**. Use the Internet to gain more information.

4 What situations do you think the British Transport police might face that require the services of a police chaplain?

5 Choose *one* of the following and write down the responsibilities you think they have towards people they come into contact with. Would their responsibilities be different if they were Christians? Why?

● Car driver.
● Supermarket owner.
● Head teacher.
● Member of your form.
● Football supporter.
● Person on the street.

Giving to charity

to think through why Christians give to charities

'My brothers and sisters, what good is it for people to say that they have faith if their actions do not prove it? Can that faith save them? Suppose there are brothers or sisters who need clothes and don't have enough to eat. What good is there in your saying to them, "God bless you! Keep warm and eat well!" – if you don't give them the necessities of life?'

(James 2:14–16)

'Jesus… said, "You need only one thing. Go and sell all you have and give the money to the poor, and you will have riches in heaven; then come and follow me."'

(Mark 10:21)

'Rich people who see a brother or sister in need, yet close their hearts against them, cannot claim that they love God. My children, our love should not be just words and talk; it must be true love, which shows itself in action.'

(1 John 3:17–18)

Rights and responsibilities

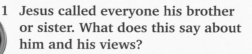

Why support a charity?

Activity

1 Jesus called everyone his brother or sister. What does this say about him and his views?

2 Read the three scripture passages on page 66, then explain how Christians are told to respond to poverty. What reasons are given?

Jesus' command in Mark's Gospel has caused Christians great problems. Only a few people, like Mother Teresa, have ever felt able to do exactly as Jesus required. Not many people decide to give up their job and family to go and look after people on the other side of the world. Society would also grind to a halt if everybody abandoned their daily life. There are, however, many ways in which Christians get involved with helping others from simply dropping coins in a collector's tin to giving their spare time to do charitable work.

When confronted by images of suffering on television or in the newspaper, many people want to help. Even if they do not belong to any particular religion, people feel that those suffering are human beings just like us. They do have a right to a decent standard of living, just as we do.

Suffering is often a matter of chance. Someone may have been unlucky enough to be born in a country with constant famines and war. It is probably our good fortune to have been born into a family, or a society, where we receive the basic necessities of life – and more. But even in this country some people suffer, through no fault of their own, from diseases that can't be cured. Other people are perfectly healthy. The idea that some of us are lucky, and some of us aren't, can inspire some non-believers to give to charity. They see it as simply being fair and trying to get rid of some of the injustices in life.

Activity

3 Make a poster to show a variety of ways people help others. Here are a few ideas to help you:

- Walking dogs for the Dogs Trust at weekends and school holidays.
- Responding to a TV campaign for a disaster fund.
- Sending charity Christmas cards.

4 Make up an acrostic poem based on the word 'CHARITY'. In an acrostic poem each new line should start with the next letter of the word 'charity'.

5 a A well-known saying, used by Christian and non-Christian alike, is: 'There but for the grace of God, go I.' What does this mean?

b Write a story where a character uses this saying.

c What implications does this saying have for Christians?

6 Decide on a good cause that could benefit from help. Give your charity a name. Write an article for a church magazine telling Christians what the cause is and why they should help. Include some scripture quotations to support your argument. Make sure you also include reasons why non-religious people might like to help.

Let's work together

Humanists say that we have evolved as a co-operative species – we need to live and work together. Very few of us could survive long or be happy without other people. Because we all depend on each other, it is sensible to treat other people as we would like to be treated ourselves.

Communities can survive and work efficiently and increase the welfare and happiness of their members, only if the people who live in them co-operate and accept certain principles, based on shared human values. These include: looking after the young and other vulnerable people; valuing truth and respecting promises; fair allocation of power and property according to some recognised system which includes merit; mutual assistance in defence and disasters; disapproval and punishment of wrongdoers; and restraints on violence and killing.

No man is an island

(A) This is a very famous line from a poem by John Donne. What do you think it means?

Many charities were started by Christians but no longer have any particular links with that religion today. The Red Cross, Oxfam, Barnados and Amnesty International were all founded by Christians. Today, these charities no longer regard themselves as Christian organisations, but rather as humanitarian organisations.

(B) Neighbours from hell.

Activity

1   Everybody in a community has a duty to act responsibly towards each other. The 'neighbours from hell' sound a bit of a joke until you experience them yourself. Design an A5 'Neighbours Charter' which gives *five* things that make a good neighbour and *five* things that make a bad neighbour. Cartoons would make people read it!

2 Research the origins of *one* charity that was founded by a Christian. Give a presentation to the class. Make sure you explain why the founder thought this issue should concern Christians.

3 Why do you think many charities that began as Christian organisations have dropped their specific links to that religion?

In recent years, charities have been formed in response to a specific human need rather than inspired by a particular religion. Members of various religions work for charities alongside people who do not believe God exists.

One charity explains how they started.

'It was a group of exasperated French doctors who lit the spark which became Médecins Sans Frontières. Frustrated and angered at the inadequacies they saw in the global response to the Biafran Crisis [in Africa] in the Seventies, they were determined to create a unity of people – medical professionals and logistics experts – who, together, could bring humanitarian aid to whoever needed it, anywhere in the world.'

Médecins Sans Frontières regard helping others as simple justice. 'There is nothing heroic about being a decent human being,' the charity's president says.

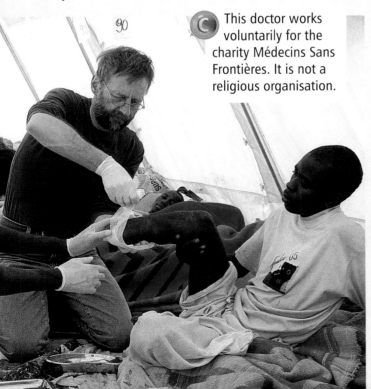

 This doctor works voluntarily for the charity Médecins Sans Frontières. It is not a religious organisation.

Band Aid, Comic Relief and Live Aid

D Sir Bob Geldof

All these charities, which have raised millions to help the starving, owe their origins to one man – Sir Bob Geldof. In 1985, Geldof watched a television report about the famine in Ethiopia. The terrible plight of the children pushed him into action and he contacted various friends in the pop world asking them to help him produce a charity record. Lots of pop stars agreed to take part for free and a recording studio gave them 24 hours free time to record and mix the record.

The record was released on 15 December and went straight to number one and sold over three million copies in five weeks, with every penny going to charity. It was the fastest-selling single of all time in the UK.

The group called themselves Band Aid. Not only did it mean a band of musicians getting together to help, but was also the name of a sticking plaster. Geldof and others were saying that the money they were raising was no more than a sticking plaster over a wound. It did not heal the whole problem of world famine.

So successful was Band Aid that a year later Live Aid followed. It was now a global response to famine and raised 10 times the amount of money.

4 Research Sir Bob Geldof's charity work and write a magazine article about this. People will be interested to know why everyone responded so generously to his appeal when he has been described as 'a scruffy, foul-mouthed individual' and 'Bob the Gob'.

5 Find out what Comic Relief has done to help people.

objective

to understand how
some Christians
take responsibility
for their religion

glossary

Adult baptism
Confirmation
Missionary
Spiritual

There often comes a time in the life of a Christian when they want to demonstrate publicly that they are taking responsibility for their religious life. In some branches of Christianity this takes the form of **adult baptism** and may involve total immersion in a small pool in the church. In the Church of England, there is a ceremony called **confirmation** when the promises made by parents and godparents on behalf of a baby are repeated by the adult themselves. This is because the adult wants to take on the responsibility for being a Christian.

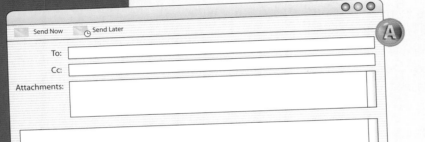

A

Hi Sarah

Thanks for your e-mail. I know you were surprised to hear I was being confirmed. It's not that I'm feeling like a goody-goody or anything. It's just that I think if you really believe in something then you ought to have the courage to stand up and say so.

After all, Jesus was prepared to stand up for what he believed in.

You sounded as though you were afraid I was going to be all holy. No, it's not that. I just want help in doing the right thing. Don't we all! But if I am confirmed, I would have other members of my church to turn to and the power of the Holy Spirit to support me. Now that's pretty special, isn't it?

Cheers

Paul

Activity

1 a Read Luke 10:3–11 and find out exactly how Jesus told his followers to behave.

   b Adapt these instructions for Paul in **A** once he has been confirmed.

2 Research: Find out what Paul will have to do to prepare for confirmation and what will happen on the day.

3 How do you react to people who want to tell you about their religion? When you form your answer bear in mind this is a free country and that you can walk away if you want to. Remember also that you might not know anything if you weren't told it by someone.

B Mark Berry is a modern-day missionary. He has been sent to the new town of Telford in Shropshire where only one in 100 goes to church.

Missionaries

Some Christians undertake their religious duties in a very public way and become **missionaries**. This is because Jesus told his followers, 'Go forth to every part of the world and proclaim the Good News to the whole creation.'

The CMS (Church Missionary Society) was founded 200 years ago to help people fulfil Jesus' command. Although in the past they worked overseas, today most of CMS's missionaries work in Britain.

In 2005, CMS placed Mark Berry in the new town of Telford where fewer than one person in 100 goes to church. Some have said this makes it one of the most ungodly places in Britain, but the locals disagree. They say going to church isn't everything and Mark Berry agreed. In his opinion it was 'not about bums on pews, not about the need to fill churches. It's… allowing people to do church their way… What I want to say is that it is not that people are less **spiritual**; rather, they think about spirituality in different ways. I want to connect with people who are spiritual but not religious… We want to be part of the conversation rather than putting ourselves away in our nice traditional stone buildings and ghettoising ourselves. This is not about being trendy. It's about giving people the opportunity to search.'

(Quotes from 'Missionary takes on tough test in darkest Telford' *The Guardian* 11 July 2005)

Activity

4 What are the people Mark Berry is talking about searching for? How can he help them find it?

5 Do you think there is any truth in Mark Berry's comment that whilst people are still spiritual, they aren't religious? You could look back to page 10 for statistics from the 2001 census to help you. Why do you think this is?

6 Design an advert Mark Berry could put in the local newspaper to let people know about his mission.

Kidz Klub is run by a Christian group called Frontline Church. They aim is to ensure every child has the opportunity to hear the Gospel. They do this though a weekly club which they say is 'packed with fun, games, prizes, panto, competitions, singing and a full Gospel presentation. The club has been described as a cross between Saturday Morning TV and a modern version of Sunday school.' Kidz Klub began in 1993 and has worked in many areas of inner-city Liverpool.

'Our aim,' they say, 'has always been to present the good news of Jesus Christ to children in a way that they can understand and in a manner that keeps their attention… Everything we do, from the warm welcome each child receives, to the fun and laughter of the games, points towards this aim. We don't just preach the love of God, we demonstrate it from the minute the first child arrives, to the minute the last child leaves.'

C These children are having fun at a Christian youth club called Kidz Klub. What sort of Christian values could they learn there?

Activity

7 Design a T-shirt for the children to wear at Kidz Klub. It needs to show this is a Christian organisation and that it is fun to be part of.

71

What can I do?

Yes, I feel sorry for her but what can I do? If I give her money for food she might spend it on drugs. That would do more harm than good.

A Official government figures estimate there are 50,000 people living on the streets of Britain. This situation concerns many Christians.

Many Christians face a dilemma when they see a homeless person begging. They know what Jesus taught and want to help, but are unsure how to go about it.

MegaBite is one charity's solution to the problem. It began life as a project in Exeter in 1991 but after it was featured on the BBC 'Food and Drink Programme' in 1997, the idea really took off. A Christian organisation working with the homeless was able to develop the project further and in 1998 MegaBite was born.

Activity

1 a As a class, consider the ways a Christian, or a group of Christians, could help people living rough.

b Why do Christians think they should get involved? Look back to pages 64–67 to remind you.

The organisers of MegaBite say:

'Many people feel uncomfortable about giving cash to people asking for help on the street, fearing that it could be spent in servicing an addiction. The action recommended by the government in response to the situation – to give time or money to a homelessness charity instead – does not solve the problem of how to help a particular individual in need. MegaBite provides a third option where people neither need to give cash nor walk by: they give MegaBite Squares and can be sure of helping in a constructive way.'

Although there is a central organisation that helps with the setting-up of such a project, each MegaBite is organised and run locally.

Activity

2 Role-play an interview between a homeless person and a Christian serving at a MegaBite food outlet.

3 Study diagram **B** that shows how this charity works, then use it to write a press release explaining how the project works and why Christians might like to get involved.

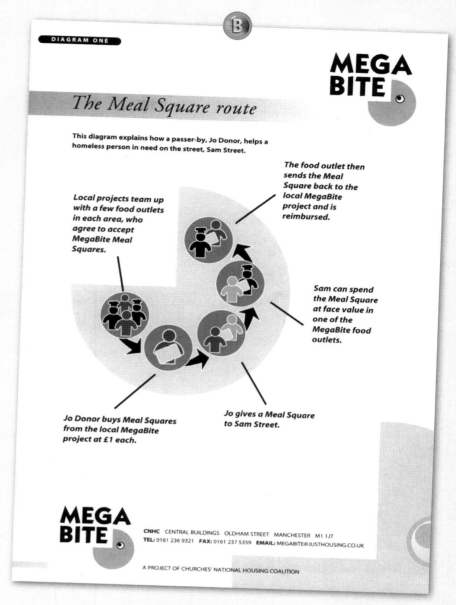

B

DIAGRAM ONE

MEGA BITE

The Meal Square route

This diagram explains how a passer-by, Jo Donor, helps a homeless person in need on the street, Sam Street.

Local projects team up with a few food outlets in each area, who agree to accept MegaBite Meal Squares.

The food outlet then sends the Meal Square back to the local MegaBite project and is reimbursed.

Sam can spend the Meal Square at face value in one of the MegaBite food outlets.

Jo Donor buys Meal Squares from the local MegaBite project at £1 each.

Jo gives a Meal Square to Sam Street.

MEGA BITE

CNHC CENTRAL BUILDINGS OLDHAM STREET MANCHESTER M1 1JT
TEL: 0161 236 9321 FAX: 0161 237 5359 EMAIL: MEGABITE@JUSTHOUSING.CO.UK

A PROJECT OF CHURCHES' NATIONAL HOUSING COALITION

C Megabite Meal voucher

£1 MEGA BITE Meal Squares

This Meal Square entitles the holder to buy food or a soft drink to the value of £1 at any of the food outlets listed overleaf. No change may be given, and Meal Squares may not be exchanged for cash. Meal Squares cannot be used to buy alcohol or tobacco.

SECURITY

Charity no 1026229
Valid until:
Serial no EX 000002

available from:
• St Petrocks - 01392 422396
• Homeless Action - 01392 430228
• Gabriel House - 01392 258899
• Esther Community - 01392 203336
• Big Issue - 01392 493372

MEGA BITE

MegaBite National Co-ordinator 0161 236 9321

Activity

4 Design a flyer that charity workers could give to homeless people explaining what the token in picture **C** is and how it can be used.

5 a How do you feel when you are confronted by a person begging in a doorway? Whose responsibility do you think it is for a situation like the one in picture **A**?

   b What would you say to someone who recommends prayer rather than action in the case of a homeless person?

Campaigning for justice

objective

to think about the ways Christians respond to homelessness

Housing Justice is a Christian charity that aims to tackle the problems of homelessness and low quality housing in the UK.

'Our vision is a society where every person has access to a home that truly meets their needs. A tough call – but we're convinced that, working together, we can make it possible. This is what we mean by Christian vision in action.

The central Christian message is that God loves us, whoever and whatever we are, and we must love him.

But Jesus commands more:
"Jesus said, 'Love the Lord your God with all your heart, with all your soul, and with all your mind.' This is the greatest and the most important commandment. The second most important commandment is like it: 'Love your neighbour as you love yourself. The whole Law of Moses and the teachings of the prophets depend on these two commandments.'"'

(Matthew 22:37–40)

HOUSING JUSTICE

Christian vision in action

A What is Housing Justice's logo saying about their intentions?

The charity also refers to Jesus' teaching in Matthew 25:35 and 40 which you can read on page 64.

They agree that everyone has different skills to offer. These might range from cooking and serving food to homeless people, working with a local group to organise help or working on a national committee. They also say:

'At the same time, churches are not simply in the business of binding up wounds – we are also called to ask awkward questions about why the wounds were inflicted in the first place. We can't avoid raising structural and political questions about housing and homelessness. We will do that best if churches, of whatever denomination, can work together.

When we work alongside homeless and badly-housed people, we are responding to the challenge to love our neighbour, we are responding to the call to put our faith into action, we are responding to the vision of a society where everyone is valued and everyone has a home.'

Activity

1 Housing Justice says it is the churches' job to ask the awkward political questions about homelessness. Do you agree? Some people say religion and politics shouldn't mix. What do you say? If it is not the responsibility of Christians to get involved in issues of homelessness, who do you think should?

2 What reasons does Housing Justice give for getting involved in homelessness?

Prayer

Our Father in heaven,
In hostels, temporary homes, alone on a park bench.
Hallowed be your name hallowed by your tenderness for all your people.
Your kingdom come to those who hunger for righteousness, to those who thirst for justice.
Your will be done as it is in heaven by those with political power and moral influence, by those who stand alongside your wounded people.
Give us this day our daily bread to share with our sisters and brothers.
Forgive us our sins as we forgive those who sin against us, our fear of risk, of loss, of sharing our wealth, our reluctance to follow where Christ leads.
Lead us not into temptation into pride, into self-righteousness; into denial of truth.
But deliver us from evil that prevents us from taking responsibility for the housing crisis.
For yours is the kingdom, the power, and the glory.
Your people, your city, your land, your glory which will transform us all.
For ever and ever
Amen

C This was part of the publicity material Housing Justice used in 2006.

STOP HOMELESSNESS

Build happiness, stop homelessness

That's the bold call of Homelessness Sunday, 29 January 2006. Homelessness Sunday is the annual opportunity to remember in worship the problems of people pushed to the margins, and to re-dedicate our work on their behalf. In 2006, the focus will be on stopping homelessness in the first place.

The resource pack
offers ideas for preventing homelessness – the approach we need to take to avoid having to mend broken lives. It offers examples of action which has worked – getting advice to people before the point of crisis; preparing people for leaving institutions; dealing with problems of anti-social behaviour. It provides materials for worship that provoke thought and strengthen resolve. It gives ideas and resources for work with children and young people.

In the Gospel for the day (Mark 1:21-28), Jesus drove out unclean spirits with authority. He brought a man whose behaviour was clearly anti-social into the community; he reached out to one from whom others recoiled. Let's use Homelessness Sunday 2006 to explore how we can do the same.

ACTIONS TO PREVENT HOMELESSNESS: TENANCY SUSTAINMENT • PROVIDE ADVICE • BUILD ENOUGH HOMES IN THE RIGHT PLACES • AFFORDABLE RENTS • DEPOSIT GUARANTEE SCHEMES • DAY CENTRES • BEFRIENDING PROGRAMMES • DRUGS AND ALCOHOL SUPPORT • SUPPORT FOR FAMILIES • STARTER PACK SCHEMES • SUPPORT IN BEREAVEMENT • TACKLING ANTI-SOCIAL BEHAVIOUR • BUDGETING ADVICE

Homelessness SUNDAY

Homelessness Sunday 2006 is organised by the Homelessness Sunday Partnership – Housing Justice in England and Wales, and Scottish Churches Housing Action.

Homelessness Sunday is supported by the major Christian denominations, Christian housing charities and others working with and for homeless people.

www.homelessness-sunday.org.uk

3 The prayer in **B** is an adaptation of the famous prayer Jesus taught his followers. You can read The Lord's Prayer in Matthew 6:9–13. What does prayer **B** ask God to do? What responsibility does it put upon Christian people?

4 The charity Housing Justice holds an annual Homelessness Sunday. Design a new poster they could use to draw attention to the problem. Make sure you explain that this is something Christians should get involved in. What type of activities could they organise for the day to raise awareness of the problem? What other activities might help to raise money for their work?

Who's responsible for the shopping?

objective

to understand the impact our decisions can have on others

glossary

Bible
Fair trade
Omnipotent

The **Bible** says 'clothe the poor' but some would say that today it is the poor who are clothing us. The bargain clothes we buy in high street stores are usually made overseas in some of the world's poorest countries. 850 million people around the world earn less than a living wage. This means they cannot afford to feed their children, send them to school or have access to safe water or sanitation.

The Christian charity Tearfund travelled to India to meet Shima. Shima is 17 and works in a clothes factory in Bangladesh, putting buttonholes in jeans and jackets. She works six days a week from 8 am till 8 or 9 pm. For that, Shima receives £4 a week. Shima lives in a slum area and her wages only provide half the money she needs to pay for basic food, healthcare and accommodation.

Tearfund is running a campaign called 'Lift the Label' to help people trapped in circumstances such as hers. They are following the Bible's call to:

'Speak up for people who cannot speak for themselves. Protect the rights of all who are helpless. Speak for them and be a righteous judge. Protect the rights of the poor and needy.' (Proverbs 31:8–9)

TEARFUND

CHRISTIAN ACTION WITH THE WORLD'S POOR

B Tearfund's logo.

A It has been said that shopping is probably where most of us have contact with the world's poor. Why is this?

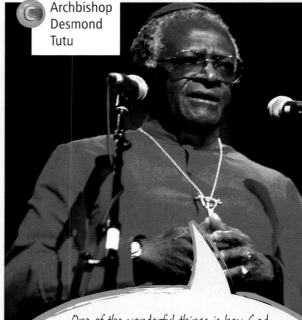

C Archbishop Desmond Tutu

*One of the wonderful things is how God depends on all of us, which is actually mind-boggling because here you have God who is **omnipotent** and yet waits on human creatures to be God's partners and collaborators. Each one of us has a contribution, each and every one of us.*

Activity

1 Who do you think is responsible for Shima's poor wages and living conditions? What would Desmond Tutu say?

2 Role-play a conversation between a Tearfund worker and someone shopping for a pair of jeans.

 Martin Luther King

Before you have finished eating your breakfast this morning you've depended on half the world. This is the way our universe is structured. We aren't going to have peace on earth until we recognise this basic fact.

3 Check whether Martin Luther King's statement is true. List everything you ate and drank before you came to school this morning – or you could list what you had for tea last night. Which countries would those products have come from?

Fair trade

Many Christians believe that we have a responsibility for our behaviour towards everyone on earth, and that includes the people who supply things for us to buy. It seems that, in order for us to enjoy cheap food and clothes, workers in other countries live and work in appalling conditions. It is particularly cheap to employ young children in poor countries. This means they never have the chance of education. Some families need to send everybody out to work so they can get enough money to survive.

Groups like the Catholic Association For Overseas Development (CAFOD), Oxfam and Christian Aid campaign to award the **fair trade** mark to products whose workers have received a fair price for their labours and just treatment from their employers. Tearfund says that when Jesus asks Christians to love their neighbour as themselves, he meant any other human being they come into contact with, and that includes through their shopping.

Traidcraft, Cafédirect and People Tree are all companies that supply goods that have been awarded the Fairtrade mark because their producers have been paid a decent wage.

'You can't leave your conscience at the check-out'

Tearfund says we should consider the impact of what we buy on the producers. This was what Jesus meant when he told his followers that 'workers should be given their pay' (Luke 10:7). Christians today think this is telling the rich West not to exploit poorer nations who do not have the same bargaining powers as them.

In another part of the New Testament, Christians are warned about exploiting the poor: '…You have piled up riches in these last days. You have not paid any wages to those who work in your fields. Listen to their complaints!'
(James 5:3–4)

Products have to be paid for, and the cheap ones often cost less because at some point someone has been paid less for their work. The voiceless are the ones who often get squeezed out of the fair wages... Buying Fairtrade says 'No' to the system that abuses others and says 'Yes' to a decent wage for a decent job. The choice is yours.

(Tearfund youth website, 2004)

 A Prayer from the Baptist Union
Our God,
Who gave commandments that guide us into paths of
justice and compassion,
Teach us what it means to make good rules,
We pray for rules to govern our trade
That can bend to serve the needs of the poor,
That are strong to contain the greed of the rich,
That will challenge the inequalities present in our world.
Make us restless for change,
Refusing to submit to political realities
Where life and death are bought in the market place,
And daring to work for the coming of your kingdom
Where the world is reshaped in the image of Christ.
In whose name we pray. Amen

4 What do you make of the situation described on these pages? Does it have anything to do with you?

5 What does Tearfund mean when they say, 'You can't leave your conscience at the check-out'? What should a Christian do about it?

objective

to consider a
Christian response
to human rights

What have human rights got to do with Christianity?

As human beings, most of us believe we are entitled to certain freedoms no matter what religion, colour or ethnic group we belong to. In 1948, after the Second World War had seen the most terrible atrocities committed against human beings by fellow humans, the United Nations Universal Declaration of Human Rights was drawn up. Although all the great nations signed up to this declaration, there are still widespread abuses of human rights. Some are on a large scale with countries treating people in appalling ways. In other instances, there are small actions which never make the headlines but cause suffering to individuals. All of these are of concern to Christians.

The Bible says:

> 'Adam named his wife Eve, because she was the mother of all human beings.'
> (Genesis 3:20)

A

> 'So God created human beings making them to be like himself.' (Genesis 1:27)

> Peter said, '…I now realise that it is true that God treats everyone on the same basis.'
> (Acts 10:34)

> 'From one human being he created all races on earth and made them live throughout the whole earth.'
> (Acts 17:26)

> 'So there is no difference between Jews and Gentiles, between slaves and free people, between men and women; you are all one in union with Christ Jesus.'
> (Galatians 3:28)

Christians have also been inspired by what Jesus said and did. His story of The Good Samaritan (Luke 10:25–37) shows that Jesus thought the way a person acted was what mattered most. In the story, the hero was a Samaritan who came from an area where Jews thought second-class citizens lived.

Activity

1 Read the scripture extracts in **A** and list *four* reasons why a Christian should be concerned about the treatment of other human beings.

Taking up Jesus' challenge

Being prepared to speak out against prejudice is a bold and dangerous thing to do. Some Christians have been brave enough to do it and a few have paid with their lives. Oscar Romero (see page 63) and Martin Luther King were both Christian ministers who publicly spoke about human rights abuse and lost their lives as a result. Their protests were not in vain. In both cases, the public outcry that followed each murder eventually led to a change in that government's attitude to human rights.

 Archbishop Desmond Tutu and Nelson Mandela are two of the greatest human rights campaigners in Africa, some people might even say in the world.

> Christian worship can never let us be indifferent to the needs of others, to the cries of the hungry, of the naked and the homeless, of the sick and the prisoner, of the oppressed and the disadvantaged.
> If it were not for faith, I am certain lots of us would have been hate-filled and bitter... But to speak of God, you must speak of your neighbour... He does not tolerate a relationship with himself that excludes your neighbour.
>
> (Archbishop Desmond Tutu)

 Activity

2 Martin Luther King is famous for his speech which started, 'I have a dream…' Find out what his dream was and what connection it has with the Christian view of human rights.

It was Archbishop Desmond Tutu's campaign against the treatment of black South Africans that helped to free Nelson Mandela from prison in 1990. Tutu always knew fighting the South African government's policy of treating black South Africans as second-class citizens would be a hard battle. What made it even harder, some thought, was that Tutu refused to use violence. As a Christian, he knew Jesus preached the message of love. 'I myself have said a number of times that I am opposed to all forms of violence,' Tutu told people. He argued that the tear gas, police dogs and bullets which the government were using on blacks was escalating the violence. 'Many blacks have despaired of peaceful change. I have warned that when people become desperate, then they will use desperate methods.'

Tutu tried peaceful means to defeat the government. At one time, he persuaded overseas countries not to buy South African goods like fruit, which was a huge export. This resulted in the government losing lots of money and getting bad publicity abroad. His brave outspoken attacks on the government's behaviour, combined with a clever campaign of civil disobedience, finally won the day. Eventually, in 1994 blacks were given the vote and Nelson Mandela became the first black, elected president.

Activity

3 a Read the quotation from Archbishop Desmond Tutu above.

   b Write a newspaper report explaining why, as a Christian, Desmond Tutu is in favour of equal human rights.

Make Poverty History

A 'I had an unbelievable life-changing experience,' Irish pop star Ronan Keating said on his return from Africa. He agreed to travel with Christian Aid so he could see for himself the conditions some people were forced to live in.

Pop legend Ronan Keating wanted to do something for human rights and, in 2004, agreed to go to Africa with Christian Aid. His intention was to increase public awareness. He met with Kofi who used to be a small-scale tomato farmer in Ghana. Kofi could no longer make a living from his land because surplus tomatoes from rich countries began to be sold in his local market which made the price of tomatoes fall. This process is known as rich countries 'dumping' cheap surplus produce on poor countries and means poor local farmers cannot compete. At the same time, the policies of rich countries prevent poor countries from stopping this or helping their own farmers. Ronan said, 'Imported tomatoes have made his old lifestyle impossible so he now works in a quarry from 6 am till it gets dark, breaking stones. He goes home with £1. Just £1 a day. This can't go on.' Ronan was appalled to learn that now Kofi had lost his farming livelihood, he struggled to pay for food and schooling for his family.

Activity

1 a What good does it do if people like Ronan Keating get involved in humanitarian campaigns?

b What do you think Ronan Keating got out of it?

c What would you like to ask Ronan Keating about his trip to Africa?

2 Design a wristband that a school could sell to raise money for a campaign to promote awareness of why farmers like Kofi have gone out of business. Remember that you have to get the message over clearly in a small space.

3 Investigate what another religion has done for the Make Poverty History campaign.

B Make Poverty History has been an extremely successful campaign that has united Christians with people of other religions and none.

As a result of the terrible poverty Ronan Keating saw on that one visit, he has continued to help Christian Aid. 'We took the Make Poverty History message to 100,000 people during my UK tour,' he said, 'and the response was overwhelming.' Not only did Ronan continue to wear his white wristband but he also took part in a march and overnight vigil to bring the Global Week of Action to a climax. 25,000 people from all across the UK marched in London to show the government and the world that they do care about the plight of other humans. The huge procession of people headed for Westminster Abbey but only 3,500 could get in. Amongst the people who spoke at the service was Ronan Keating and his message was, 'If we stick together and shout loudly enough we will make a difference.'

As well as at Westminster Abbey, there was another all-night vigil at **Methodist** Central Hall in Westminster, where Radiohead lead singer Thom Yorke performed. Outside, thousands of people processed around Parliament Square, past Downing Street and down Whitehall before holding a minute's silence. Even at 6.30 the next morning there were still 10,000 people who had kept an all-night vigil, then gathered in Parliament Square amidst a blaze of cheers, banners and whistles ready for the final procession.

Christian Aid has taken many approaches to raising awareness of the poverty of people in the developing world. Not only have they organised marches like the one shown in picture **B**, but they have encouraged supporters to write to the prime minister telling him of their concerns about world poverty. One postcard might have seemed a drop in the ocean but in fact, in 2003, Tony Blair received so many thousands that he felt obliged to write an official response to Christian Aid campaigners. MPs too spoke of bulging postbags on this subject. So the peaceful, persistent approach has helped to raise the profile of world poverty and, it is hoped, will lead to a solution.

C Charity wristbands have proved an easy but successful way of raising money and publicity for good causes.

Action!

The life and teachings of Jesus have convinced Christians that they should not stand by and allow the abuse of human rights. Jesus said:

'[God] has sent me to proclaim liberty to the captives and recovery of sight to the blind; to set free the oppressed and announce that the time has come when the Lord will save his people.'

(Luke 4:18–19)

This passage has inspired many Christians to work for justice for prisoners of conscience.

The way Christians confront the problem differs. Some believe in working through prayer, others believe in direct action.

Salisbury Cathedral has a chapel dedicated to prisoners who have suffered for their beliefs. It is called the Prisoner of Conscience Chapel and picture **A** shows the candle which stands prominently in the corner.

A This candle burns in the Prisoner of Conscience Chapel at Salisbury Cathedral.

The candle has many symbolic features which help Christians to meditate as they pray. The design is based on the logo of Amnesty International, a charity which campaigns against human rights abuse. The burning candle in the middle reminds Christians of the light of Jesus that shines even in prison. The barbed wire represents torture and reminds Christians of the crown of thorns that was rammed down on Jesus' head before he was crucified. The spikes represent the nails that were hammered into Jesus' hands to fix him to the cross. The inspiration for the sculpture came from John's Gospel:

'The light shines in the darkness, and the darkness has never put it out.'

(John 1:5)

Peter Benenson (who died in 2005) is best known as the founder of Amnesty International. Amnesty, based in London, is the world's largest independent human rights organisation with 1.8 million members and supporters. Although Peter Benenson was a Christian and a convert to Roman Catholicism, Amnesty is a non-religious organisation. They campaign for justice for everyone who has been imprisoned or tortured for their opinions, no matter what religion, colour or race they are. These people are called prisoners of conscience because they have been true to their conscience and stood by their views, no matter how unpopular these were with their government. These are people who have been prepared to suffer for what they believe to be right.

Amnesty International works in two main ways:
1 By raising awareness of human rights.
2 By focusing on specific cases and opposing them.

Today, they say that the biggest threat to human rights occurs in wars. 'People are now more likely to become victims of abuse because of who they are, rather than for what they think, say or do.'

Peter Benenson also founded the Association of Christians Against Torture (ACAT) along with the British Council of Churches and the Religious Society of Friends. This group says: 'We seek to increase awareness in the Churches and among Christians of the widespread and evil use of torture and the need, for reasons of Christian faith, to campaign for its abolition.' Like Amnesty, ACAT sends cards and letters of support to prisoners. They differ from Amnesty because they use prayer as part of their work. 'It is important to pray for individuals by name,' ACAT says. 'Many prisoners become aware that they are upheld in prayer and are given courage in their adversity.'

Activity

1 Write a brief prayer that a member of ACAT could use.

2 Design material to go on a Christian website explaining why Christians should concern themselves with prisoners of conscience. Indicate how Christians could help.

3 Discuss the reasons why some Christians favour prayer and others direct action in the fight against human rights abuse. What do you think would be most helpful?

4 Christians argue that Jesus himself was a prisoner of conscience. Look at the explanation of this term on these pages and write a paragraph explaining how this claim could be justified.

5 Design a postcard that could be sent to a prisoner of conscience. Choose a picture to inspire them to go on one side and write something appropriate on the other. Bear in mind that the prisoner may not be a Christian.

Amnesty International is famous for its letter-writing campaign. One trade union leader imprisoned in the Dominican Republic said:

'I was being kept naked in an underground cell. When the first 200 letters came, the guards gave me back my clothes. Then the next 200 letters came, and the prison director came to see me… The letters kept coming; 3,000 of them. The President was informed and he said, "How is it a trade union leader like you has so many friends all over the world?" …and he told them to let me go.'

Assessment for Unit 2

'There was once a man who was going down from Jerusalem to Jericho when robbers attacked him, stripped him, and beat him up, leaving him half dead. It so happened that a priest was going down that road; but when he saw the man, he walked on by, on the other side. In the same way a Levite also came along, went over and looked at the man, and then walked on by, on the other side. But a Samaritan who was travelling that way came upon the man, and when he saw him, his heart was filled with pity. He went over to him, poured oil and wine on his wounds and bandaged them; then he put the man on his own animal and took him to an inn, where he took care of him. The next day he took out two silver coins and gave them to the innkeeper. "Take care of him," he told the innkeeper, "and when I come back this way, I will pay you whatever else you spend on him."

(Luke 10:30–35)

These questions test different sets of skills in RE. Which skills do you need to work on? Choose the level you need and work through the tasks set.

Level 3

- Give *two* ways in which the person in the photograph is behaving like the Good Samaritan.
- Why might a Christian give extra money to charity at Christmas?
- Why do you spend more money on other people at Christmas than you do at other times of the year?

Level 4

- Give *two* ways in which the parable of The Good Samaritan inspires Christians to behave today.
- Explain why it is important for Christians to have a religious marriage ceremony rather than a civil one. What sort of responsibilities are they choosing to undertake in the Christian ceremony?
- Describe an occasion when you chose to do something for someone else and got nothing out of it. What made you do it?

Level 5

- Explain why some Christians believe they should take responsibility for the welfare of people they have never met.
- One Christian Aid worker said that the Good Samaritan's help came with no strings attached and he didn't even expect a thank you card. Explain how Jesus showed the same sort of unconditional love. How do modern Christians try to copy this?
- Why do you think Christians get involved in fighting human rights abuse? Do you consider it matters very much if it happens in a far away country or even if it happened here? Explain your reasons.

Level 6

- Explain why some Christians feel it is their duty to speak out against injustice. Do you think it achieves anything worthwhile if the person ends up getting murdered?
- Compare the way a Christian makes decisions about right and wrong actions, with the way a non-religious person decides. What sorts of things guide your decisions about right and wrong actions?
- Explain what Jesus was trying to teach his followers by choosing the characters he did in the parable of The Good Samaritan. What do you find the most shocking part of the story? Why?

We're not on our own!

Life's rubbish

- Spend a few moments studying this picture in detail.
- How many people appear to be 'working' on this rubbish tip? What is their age? What is their gender?
- Where do they live? What do you think they are looking for? What could they do with it? Why is this happening?
- Create a mind map of all the issues this picture raises.

What's the problem?

 A Distribution of wealth around the globe.

NORTH AMERICA

Pacific Ocean

Atlantic Ocean

SOUTH AMERICA

Fact file

- 826 million people on earth are undernourished.

- 20% of the world's population do not have access to safe drinking water.

- Average income in Switzerland is 80 times higher than in South Asia.

- 30,000 children die every day from illnesses that could be prevented or cured.

- Over one billion people lack basic shelter.

- One in five adults in the world can't read. 98% of them live in the developing world.

- 40% of the world do not have access to electricity.

- One-third of the food bought in Britain lands up in the dustbin.

- 20% of the world's population consume 70% of the world's grain (mostly fed to animals).

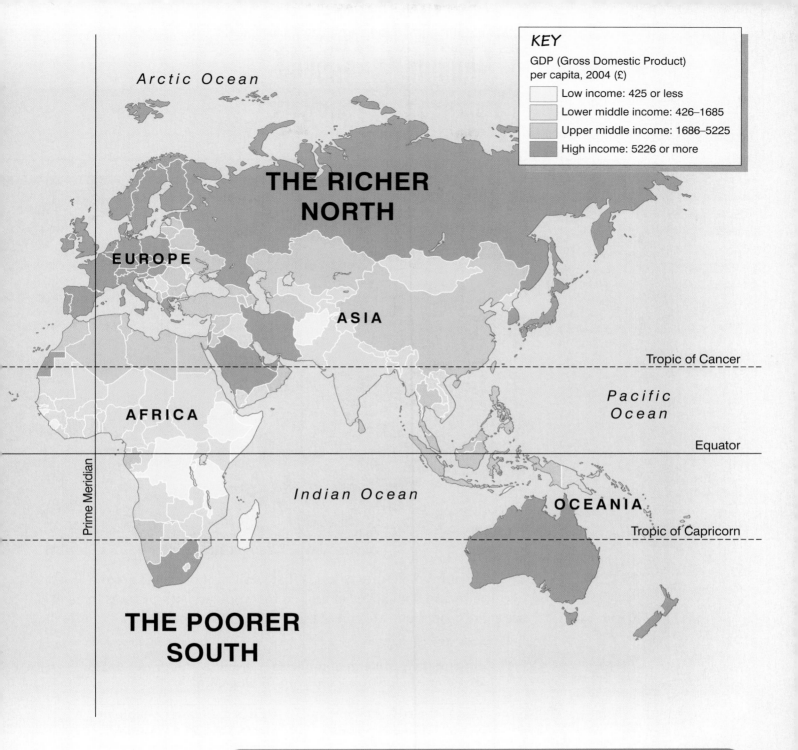

KEY

GDP (Gross Domestic Product) per capita, 2004 (£)

Low income: 425 or less
Lower middle income: 426–1685
Upper middle income: 1686–5225
High income: 5226 or more

Arctic Ocean

THE RICHER
NORTH

EUROPE

ASIA

Tropic of Cancer

Pacific
Ocean

AFRICA

Equator

Prime Meridian

Indian Ocean

OCEANIA

Tropic of Capricorn

THE POORER
SOUTH

Activity

1   It has been said that in the twenty-first century we are better off than we have ever been. Poverty is a thing of the past. Use map **A** and the fact file, along with any other information you can research, to write your view of this statement. Give some examples to prove your point.

2   Use newspaper headlines, magazine pictures and other information to create a poster that shows the big divide in the world between those who have and those who don't have.

For richer for poorer

 A Aid worker in Africa.

It is evident from pictures **A** and **B** that wealth is not spread around evenly either in our society or around the world. In both pictures there are some people who are considerably richer than others.

1 Compare the people in both pictures **A** and **B** and draw a table like the one below to record your findings.

Things the richer people in pictures **A** and **B** possess	Things the poorer people in pictures **A** and **B** possess

When you compare the state of the poorer people in each picture, you will see another vast difference again. The one in picture **A** has absolutely nothing and is unlikely to have access to any medical aid, education or welfare benefits in the country they live in. The poorer people in picture **B** are likely to have somewhere to live, have received a free education, free healthcare and have access to many more facilities and benefits in the community they live in.

 Wealthy celebrity with her fans.

Why should I bother?

A Christian, or member of another faith group, would have plenty of reasons why they should bother about people in absolute poverty. What about someone who doesn't believe God exists? Is there any reason for them to be concerned about poverty?

The Humanists would say 'Yes'. Just because they do not have a religious book or a leader to give out rules, it doesn't mean they don't have any strong beliefs. The Humanists' Golden Rule is that you should treat others as you would like to be treated yourself. They say that we are all members of the human race and it would be unjust to leave others to suffer. Helping the poor is simply the right thing to do, they say.

There is another argument. If we don't do anything and people continue to suffer, this will lead to hatred and often wars. Wars, even in remote countries, end up having an effect on us. Trade gets disrupted and communities are destroyed as large numbers of people move around in search of a better and safer existence. In the end, their suffering affects us all.

The charities that exist to help the poor in Britain, and in the developing world, are run by people who share a concern for the plight of the poor. Although a charity like Christian Aid is clearly rooted in Christian principles, it helps everyone regardless of their faith in the same way as Oxfam, Action Aid and Save the Children does.

Poverty is relative. It all depends where you are standing.

People, like the boy in picture **A**, with nothing at all who struggle to survive are in **absolute poverty**. This sort of poverty is not seen in Britain because the state can help the poorest members of society. It does exist in the developing world where state help is often non-existent.

The poorer people in picture **B** are in **relative poverty** when you compare them to the celebrity in the picture. Poverty in this case is just an uneven distribution of wealth which we do see in the western world.

Activity

2 a List the reasons why a non-religious person should help the poor. Add any other reasons of your own to those given here.

 b How would their reasons differ from a religious person's?

3 Role-play an interview between a person with a collecting tin outside the supermarket and a non-religious passer-by being asked for money.

4 List *nine* things the poor person in picture **A** is lacking. Arrange these in a diamond nine to show the order of importance.

Can you have a rich Christian?

glossary

Evangelical
Gospels
Methodist
Old Testament

Jesus knew only too well that money mattered to people and, at the same time, it caused them problems. In fact, the **Gospels** have recorded more of Jesus' teachings about money than about heaven. The only problem is that Christians are divided about the meaning of these teachings.

Jesus told this parable to explain how foolish it is to let money rule your life:

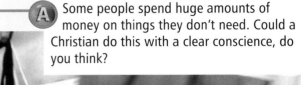

A Some people spend huge amounts of money on things they don't need. Could a Christian do this with a clear conscience, do you think?

'…There was once a rich man who had land which bore good crops. He began to think to himself, "I haven't anywhere to keep all my crops. What can I do? This is what I will do," he told himself; "I will tear down my barns and build bigger ones, where I will store my corn and all my other goods. Then I will say to myself, Lucky man! You have all the good things you need for many years. Take life easy, eat, drink and enjoy yourself!" But God said to him, "You fool! This very night you will have to give up your life; then who will get all these things you have kept for yourself?"'

(Luke 12:16–20)

'No one can be a slave of two masters; he will hate one and love the other; he will be loyal to one and despise the other. You cannot serve both God and money.' (Matthew 6:24)

'…Sell all you have and give the money to the poor, and you will have riches in heaven… It is much harder for a rich person to enter the Kingdom of God than for a camel to go through the eye of a needle.'

(Luke 18:22 and 25)

Activity

1 Write a modern-day version of the story Jesus told in Luke 12:16–20 and call it, 'You can't take it with you when you go!'

2 Would a Christian find the shopping scene like the one in picture **A** acceptable? Take into consideration the extracts from scriptures when making your decision.

3 Do you feel uneasy when you see people spending huge sums of money on luxury items? Do you think they have any responsibility to help those with nothing? Give reasons to support your answer.

- Some modern Christians believe that if you have earned your money fairly and have been generous to those in need, you are entitled to enjoy your money. They point out that when Jesus spoke of the difficulty of a camel passing through the eye of needle he went on to say, 'What is impossible for man is possible for God' (Matthew 18:22–26). These Christians argue that if everybody gave away their money, it would not solve the problem of poverty, only create more problems. What do you think?

Activity

4 'There is no such thing as a rich Christian.' Do you agree?

5 Christians were angry when the former prime minister, Margaret Thatcher, said, 'No one would remember the Good Samaritan if he only had good intentions. He had money as well.'

   a Work out what Margaret Thatcher meant by reading the story in Luke 10:30–37.

   b Would the Samaritan's lack of money have made the story pointless? Would his love and compassion towards the injured man count for anything?

   c Do you think money is the most important factor in a situation like this? Why?

What different Christians have said about wealth

- John Wesley, who founded the **Methodist** Church, gave this practical advice: 'Earn all you can; save all you can; give all you can.' How helpful do you think this approach is to life in the twenty-first century? Would it solve the problem of world poverty? What guidance might it offer to a Christian who was unsure whether or not they should play the lottery?

- Some Christians believe they should copy the lifestyle of Jesus, who owned nothing. The nun, Mother Teresa, gave up all her possessions and worked to help the poor. Her work made a big difference to the lives of those she helped and inspired hundreds more to help the poor. Yet she owned nothing, not even the clothes she wore.

- Archbishop Desmond Tutu (whose story appears on page 79) said, 'The church that is in solidarity with the poor can never be a wealthy church.' What does this mean? Do you think Tutu would agree with a richly-decorated church building?

Multi-millionaire British car importer Robert Edmiston is an **evangelical** Christian. He says:

'God is interested in character and in the attitude of our heart. In past centuries, poverty was elevated because Jesus himself was poor. In earlier times, wealth was seen as a blessing of God and many great **Old Testament** figures were wealthy and did great things with their wealth, so we need to recover the balance. It's what we do with the wealth which really counts.'

(Adapted from *The Sunday Times*, 6 February 2005)

Robert Edmiston is planning to give £300 million to charity before he dies.

This makes uncomfortable reading!

People can get very 'up-tight' about money matters. There are those who say this has got nothing to do with religion, it is politics and Christians should not get involved in politics. When Archbishop Desmond Tutu was told religion and politics don't mix, he said, 'Does it say anywhere that God is not interested too much in what happens from Monday to Saturday but only in what happens on Sunday?' What do you think?

I WAS HUNGRY
    and you fed your animals with my food.

I WAS HUNGRY
    and your transnationals planted your winter
    tomatoes on our best land.

I WAS HUNGRY
    but you wouldn't give up your
    steak from South America.

I WAS HUNGRY
    but you turned our sugar cane
    and manioc into fuel for your cars.

I WAS HUNGRY
    but the waste from your
    factories is poisoning the
    fishing grounds of the earth.

I WAS HUNGRY
    but with your money you bought up my food.

(from *Whose World?*)

KEEP OFF

BUTTER

GRAIN

MEAT

miói

B

'Two-thirds of the world do not have enough to eat while the other third is trying to lose weight.'

'Sharing God's Planet', 2005

1 Using headlines and pictures from newspapers and magazines, make a poster to show the meaning of the words in **B**.

2 a What point does cartoon **A** make? Think about the relative size of everything in the picture when working out your answer.

 b Choose *one* of the 'I was hungry' statements to examine. Do further research (the geography department may be helpful) to get some facts and figures to test the truth of the statement. Report your findings back to the rest of the class.

 c Go through each of the six points and explain exactly what it says is happening and why each is leading to hunger for some people.

3 Draw your own cartoon to illustrate one of the 'I was hungry' points being made.

4 Consider these two statements by Christians.

 ● Mother Teresa said, 'You must give what it costs you – make a sacrifice, go without something you like, that your gift may have value before God. Then you will be truly brothers and sisters to the poor who are deprived of even the things they need.'

 ● The Orthodox Christian Church says, 'Just as a shepherd will in times of greatest hazard lay down his life for his flock, so human beings may need to forego part of their wants and needs in order that the survival of the natural world can be assured. This is a new situation – a new challenge.'

 a What are these Christians saying? Compare the reasons they give for this. How do these differ?

 b Would you agree with these two ideas? What would people who disagree with you say?

 c What does the poem in cartoon A require people to give up in order that the rest of the world can eat? Is this fair?

93

Christianity and homelessness

A With a partner, work out why you think the people in these pictures needed the help of the Church Housing Trust for somewhere to live.

Jesus said:

'I was hungry and you fed me, thirsty and you gave me a drink; I was a stranger and you received me in your homes, naked and you clothed me; I was sick and you took care of me, in prison and you visited me... whenever you did this for one of the least important of these members of my family, you did it for me!'

(Matthew 25:35–36 and 40)

The Church Housing Trust is a charity dedicated to the rehabilitation and resettlement of homeless people of all ages and backgrounds. They aim to tackle the underlying issues that cause homelessness, rather than look for quick fixes.

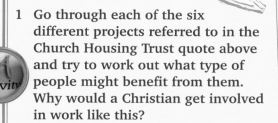

> *Our ultimate goal is to help homeless people regain their independence and resettle in the community, by supporting residents in over 50 projects including hostels, move-on housing, day centres, winter shelters, women's refuges and mother and baby projects.*

Activity

1 Go through each of the six different projects referred to in the Church Housing Trust quote above and try to work out what type of people might benefit from them. Why would a Christian get involved in work like this?

- Church Housing Trust's Welfare Fund helps people from the day they first arrive at a hostel, for example by the provision of a 'Welcome Pack' of food and toiletries.

- They support a range of initiatives to prepare residents for independent living. These include: life skills training (e.g. cooking and budgeting); funding training rooms and equipment; providing grants for residents to attend training courses; and clothing for attending job interviews.

- They help residents who are moving on from the hostels by providing grants to purchase essential items of furniture or kitchen equipment. This is a life-line to people with no resources of their own, who might otherwise move into a completely bare flat.

CASE STUDY

Claire is a 17 year old who lived at Bracken Court in Leeds for 10 months. She was involved with a drug addict and her parents asked her to leave her family home because they could not cope with her behaviour. When she became pregnant she moved into a council property, but the resettlement worker remained in regular contact with her as there were worries that she could not cope with the baby. Fortunately Claire has proved to be an excellent mother. Both Mum and baby are doing well, the father of the child has moved in and Claire has re-established her relationship with her parents. Once again, Church Housing Trust was able to help by providing a grant towards the cost of necessities such as a cooker, fridge and carpets for the flat.

Activity

2 What would you include in the £150 Welcome Pack for Claire when she first moved into the council flat?

3 Which life skills training would you recommend the Church Housing Trust helped Claire with? Why?

HIV and AIDS

glossary

Pandemic

1 As a class, consider what problems a poor country would face if most of the population became ill and died before the age of 40?

The problem of HIV/AIDS

HIV/AIDS is so acute in the developing world that it is called a **pandemic**. 95% of people with HIV/AIDS live in the developing world where there is great poverty. Although there is no cure for HIV/AIDS, it can be controlled with strong drugs, adequate food and clean water and sanitation. The spread of the disease can also be slowed by education. This all costs money which people in these countries often do not have. The drugs cost around £250 a year for a person who probably earns £1.40 a day if they are able to work.

Christian Aid says:

HIV/AIDS is threatening to undermine much of the progress that has been made in recent years in such fields as healthcare, education and agriculture in the world's poorest countries. It impacts on the whole of society, by causing the ill health and death of the main breadwinners and of the parents of the next generation.

Money has to be spent on healthcare, people are forced to give up jobs to care for sick members of their family and children are being forced to go out to work at an ever younger age to support their family.

HIV/AIDS is wiping out the work force. Businesses and schools are suffering as employees die. It is estimated that in Zambia five teachers die of HIV/AIDS every day.

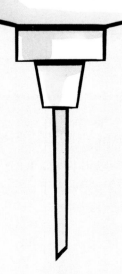

A **Fact file**

Number of people living with HIV/AIDS
- Sub-Saharan Africa, 25.8 million.
- Latin America, 1.8 million.
- South and South-East Asia, 7.4 million.
- The Caribbean, 0.3 million.
- Rest of the world, 5 million.
- 8,500 people die as a result of HIV/AIDS every day.
- Over 6,000 children are orphaned every day as a result of HIV/AIDS.
- 13,500 people are infected with HIV/AIDS every day.

The average life-expectancy of people living with HIV/AIDS in some of the most affected countries has dropped from around 60 years to 40 years and continues to fall. There is currently no vaccine available and this remains an enormous challenge.

What is the Christian attitude to HIV/AIDS?

Because Jesus said:

'…I have come in order that you might have life – life in all its fullness'

(John 10:10)

his followers believe they should try to assist people living with HIV/AIDS. Jesus also met and helped people who had been rejected by society and because people living with HIV/AIDS are frequently rejected, Christians try to follow Jesus' example.

> 2 Remind yourself of the story of The Lost Son in Luke 15:11–32. What parts of this story might inspire Christians to help HIV/AIDS sufferers who have been rejected by their community?

Archbishop Desmond Tutu said Christians should be concerned about AIDS:

> We should not want those living with HIV to be the modern equivalent of the Biblical leper who had to carry a bell and a sign saying, 'I am unclean'. They are not unclean. We should embrace them physically and emotionally as members of our community.

Christian Aid

This charity is funding many healthcare projects in poor communities and providing support to orphans. In the north of Zambia, they are working with a local Catholic organisation to train nurses and health workers who can help the chronically ill in their homes. In Jamaica, they have supported a project that teaches young people about HIV/AIDS through dance, music and drama. In Brazil, there has been support for a young people's theatre group that performs educational plays to other young people.

B Celestine from the Democratic Republic of Congo has been helped by a project set up by 'Fondation Femme Plus' (FFP) and funded by Christian Aid.

Fifteen women living with HIV/AIDS were given a camera and films, then taught how to use them. They were encouraged to capture images portraying the reality of life with AIDS. Exhibitions of their work have been used to educate others and the project has given the women a method of earning a living because they can earn £140 a film, photographing family weddings and events in their locality.

Celestine explains:

> I am a widow with seven children. Our house is in a bad condition. For the time being, FFP helps me. This means I can get food. My husband's family rejected me, and now I have to take care of the children and pay for school fees. But I'm very happy with this project, as are my children. I can earn money and I can educate other people. We should look after people who are living with HIV/AIDS, not reject them. We should eat with them and wash their clothes for them.

> 3 Produce an A5 leaflet Christian Aid could use to encourage people to donate to help their work with HIV/AIDS.

Why care? Y Care International

Activity

1 Use the material from this leaflet to plan a TV campaign to raise money for the charity. You will need to be clear about the aims of their work. You will need to refer to the reasons Christians do this sort of work. These can be found on pages 66–67, 78–79, 82–83 and 90–91 of this book. Consider whether you would like to include a brief interview with someone. Who would that be? Y Care International's website, www.ycare.org.uk, could also give you useful information.

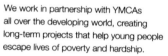

About Y Care International

Y Care International is the development and relief agency for the YMCA in the UK & Ireland. It was co-founded in 1984 by Terry Waite CBE. The YMCA is one of the biggest Christian charities in the world, working with young people in over 120 countries.

We work in partnership with YMCAs all over the developing world, creating long-term projects that help young people escape lives of poverty and hardship.

It is our belief that transforming the lives of young people will improve a world increasingly affected by injustice, poverty and hunger.

Hundreds of children live on the streets

With your help, they won't die there

For thousands of children in Colombia's capital city, Bogota, every day is a fight for survival.

They have no homes, no families and no way out. These youngsters live on the streets, scratching around in rubbish bins or begging for food and sleeping in discarded storage bags. They are constantly frightened of being violently attacked, kidnapped and tortured, or simply starving to death.

But there is hope. Our YMCA centre has given many children like Salvadore safe new lives, far away from the dangerous and violent streets of Bogota.

Y CARE INTERNATIONAL
EFFECTIVE AID THROUGH YMCAs WORLDWIDE

Registered Charity No. 1109789

All photographs of children, except front cover are courtesy of www.flickr.com/photos/beja-flor

2 Y Care International works through the worldwide YMCA movement (YMCA stands for Young Men's Christian Association). Research the YMCA movement in Britain. Find out where your nearest YMCA is and who it helps. Report your findings back to the class.

3 Y Care International provides immediate help to street children and then long-term support to help them find a better way of life. Write a magazine article about Y Care International explaining about both types of assistance.

Salvadore's story

Salvadore fled to Bogota after a savage beating from his stepfather left him bleeding from his ears. He was just 8 years old when he arrived to swell the ranks of 'los desachables' or the disposables, which is how the homeless children of the city are known.

Salvadore found life on the streets brutal. If he ate, it was rotten food from bins. If he slept, it was fitfully, in cold alleyways. Gangs roamed the city at night, kidnapping and murdering street children and some of Salvadore's friends had recently disappeared.

Luckily, he was found by an outreach worker who encouraged him to visit the YMCA centre. Here, Salvadore was given a hot bath, a real bed and three meals a day for 10 days. During that time, we arranged somewhere safe for him to stay and his return to school.

£30 buys a street child
everything they need
to survive

£30 can do
so much

Every year, 2,500 homeless young people visit our YMCA centre, in Bogota. When they arrive, they are frightened, hungry and dirty. We give them a bed to sleep in, a hot bath and three meals every day they are at the centre.

On average, it takes 10 days to find a child somewhere safe to stay. And while they are with us, they will receive all the advice and encouragement they need to stay off the streets for good.

Although we have already helped thousands of street children turn their lives around, there are still many more who need our help.

An education

Most street children are forced to drop out of school. As part of our long-term support, we help them catch up and return to education.

A safe place to sleep

Many street children have never seen a proper bed. While they stay with us, they will sleep safely for the first time in months.

3 meals a day

Children haven't eaten properly for weeks when they arrive at the YMCA. We give them three meals each day of their stay.

Please fill in the card enclosed. Your message will show these children that someone cares.

Please give just £30 and help us take a child off the streets for good.

Why bother with the environment?

Fact file

- Global snow cover has shrunk by 10% since the 1960s.
- Sea levels rose between 10–20 cm in the twentieth century.
- 27,000 died in Europe in the 2003 heat wave, **global warming** is thought to have caused that heat wave.
- The 10 warmest years have occurred since 1990.
- The UK has 1% of the world's population but produces 2.5% of the world's carbon dioxide.

Fact file

- 60% of the Great Barrier Reef was damaged by coral bleaching in 2002 because of rising sea temperatures.
- One in four fish caught is thrown back into the sea dead or dying.
- 80% of sea pollution comes from land-based activities.
- The contents of 21 million barrels of oil are estimated to land up in the oceans every year.
- Two million seabirds die every year from eating or getting entangled in waste plastic.

- 50 species become extinct every day due to tropical **deforestation**.

- 25% of mammals and 12% of birds are likely to become extinct in the next few decades as warmer conditions change their habitat.

- Polar bears could vanish within 70 years as the Arctic sea ice melts.

- Orang-utans will be extinct in 12 years if palm oil production is not controlled.

- An acre of rainforest that is felled contains 1,500 plant species.

Fact file

- Every year, half a million people in the world are poisoned by pesticides.

- 24,000 people in the UK die because of air pollution, mainly due to traffic fumes.

- Between 7–20% of cancers are thought to be caused by pollution.

- 90% of UK energy comes from burning fossil fuels.

Activity

1 Using the pictures and their fact files, make a note of what each problem is highlighting.

2 Design a poster that shows some of the environmental problems in the sea, earth and sky. You do not have to use the ones that have been shown here.

3 Consider how much humans have caused the problems on these pages. Would our lifestyle suffer much if we changed our ways?

Non-religious concern for the environment

Many people are concerned about the future of our planet. They argue that it is simple common sense because our survival as a species depends on the survival of the earth.

One early person to speak about this was Chief Seattle, a native American chief from the Suquamish tribe. In 1854 he said:

> Man did not weave the web of life – he is merely a strand in it. Whatever he does to the web, he does to himself.

Humanists, who do not believe there is any evidence for the existence of God, are firmly convinced that human beings should care for the environment. They would not automatically blame science and technology for our environmental problems. In fact, they say, it is thanks to biologists that we know so much about environmental problems.

Here are some Humanist views:

A Many people who do not belong to any organised religion have concern for the future of the earth. This was the idea behind this garden design.

B Humanists appreciate the happiness and inspiration that contact with nature and animals can bring. Life on earth is both beautiful and valuable, and we should do more to preserve habitats, species and ways of life that are being destroyed by the over-exploitation of natural resources and wilderness areas. We need these for materials, food, fuel, and as a source of genetic diversity for artificial breeding programmes – many of our medicines, for example, have been developed from natural materials, and there may be many useful ones that we have not yet discovered. And bio-geo-chemical cycles are vital for life on the planet – for example, tropical rainforests have been called the 'lungs' of the planet, and it might be hard for the planet to manage without them. In permitting the loss or destruction of natural resources we may inadvertently be damaging ourselves – we don't always know what might be important or useful in the future, and so should preserve as much bio-diversity as possible, just in case. It is difficult or impossible to protect or reintroduce species once their habitat has been destroyed, and thousands of species become extinct every year, impossible to revive.

Greenpeace

Greenpeace is a non-profit-making organisation that uses non-violent campaigning methods to expose global environmental problems and their causes.

Greenpeace has organised campaigns:

- for the protection of oceans and ancient forest
- for the phasing out of fossil fuels and the promotion of renewable energies in order to stop climate change
- for the elimination of toxic chemicals
- against the release of genetically-modified organisms into nature
- for nuclear disarmament and an end to nuclear contamination.

Activity

1 a What reasons do Humanists give for being concerned about the environment in **B**?

  b Do you agree with them or are there any you would question?

2 There are similarities in the words of Chief Seattle and in the Humanists' argument in **B**. What are they? What specific example could be used to prove this?

3 Using the information from leaflet **C**, prepare a short talk about the *four* issues Greenpeace are concerned about.

LOVE HATE

Do you share our passion?

LOVE HATE

Just £3 a month will help **GREENPEACE** bring about change

C A Greenpeace campaign leaflet.

objective

to understand the Christian teachings about the environment and the way they are interpreted

glossary

Bible
Holy Communion
Roman Catholic
Stewardship

Christian teachings about creation and stewardship

The scriptures say:

'O Lord, our Lord your greatness is seen in all the world!'
(Psalm 8:1)

'The world and all that is in it belong to the Lord; the earth and all who live on it are his.'
(Psalm 24:1)

'Then the Lord God placed the man in the Garden of Eden to cultivate it and guard it.'
(Genesis 2:15)

'Then God said, "And now we will make human beings; they will be like us and resemble us. They will have power over the fish, the birds, and all animals, domestic and wild, large and small." So God created human beings, making them to be like himself. He created them male and female, blessed them, and said, "Have many children, so that your descendants will live all over the earth and bring it under their control. I am putting you in charge of the fish, the birds, and all the wild animals."'
(Genesis 1:26–29)

Although Jesus did not teach about environmental issues, Christians believe his words in Luke's Gospel (12:6) give them an insight into the importance of all aspects of creation.

'Aren't five sparrows sold for two pennies? Yet not one sparrow is forgotten by God.'
(Luke 12:6)

1 How could Jesus' words about sparrows in Luke 12:6 help Christians understand environmental issues?

2 Jesus also said, '...You are worth much more than many sparrows!' (Luke 12:7) Do you think that might change a Christian's concern for the environment?

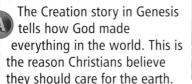

A The Creation story in Genesis tells how God made everything in the world. This is the reason Christians believe they should care for the earth.

Stewardship

The **Bible** says that God made every living thing in existence. It also says that, although God put humans in charge, the earth's resources still belong to God and people only manage them for the real owner, God. This is called **stewardship**. Human life is short in comparison with the lifespan of the planet and humans must hand back the planet to its real owner in good condition.

The Pope, head of the **Roman Catholic** Church, gave his followers these five principles:

1 The earth and all life on it is a gift from God given to us to share and develop, not to dominate and exploit.

2 Our actions have consequences for the rights of others and for the resources of the earth.

3 The goods of the earth and the beauties of nature are to be enjoyed and celebrated as well as consumed.

4 We have the responsibility to create a balanced policy between consumption and conservation.

5 We must consider the welfare of future generations in our planning for, and utilisation of, the earth's resources.

3 a Choose *one* of the five principles above and put it in your own words.

   b Would any of the scripture extracts support these five principles?

   c How could a Christian put these principles into practice?

   d Do you think principles 1 and 3 cancel each other out?

   e Would you agree with all the Pope's principles or can you see any difficulties they might cause for the world of the twenty-first century?

B **This prayer was composed for Eco-Congregation**

Creating God, you have given us a vision of a new heaven and a new earth
Resources conserved
Earth tended
Atmosphere cleansed
Trees planted
Injustice ended
Oceans teeming
Nations at peace

Creator, Redeemer, Sustainer
Alert nations, Enthuse churches.
Receive our commitment and so entwine our lives with Your purpose
Earth and heaven will then sing of your glory.
Amen

In 2005, the Archbishop of Canterbury, head of the Church of England, urged the church to work towards a greener world. The report he commissioned, called 'Sharing God's Planet', warned that the world's climate is close to a 'tipping point'. 'The sudden changes that would occur in weather systems, the fertility of the soil, the water and the world of living creatures if this tipping point were reached could be devastating.' The Archbishop said Christians must adopt a 'sustainable consumption' and recognise it is their duty to 'celebrate and care for every part of God's creation'.

At a local level, the Church of England encourages churches to recycle, share cars, sell fair trade products at church fêtes and use organic bread and wine for **Holy Communion**.

4 Write the script for a religious broadcast that tells Christians why they should care for God's planet. Give them a few practical suggestions as to how they might play their part.

5 It is obvious what is going on in picture **C** but the reasons behind the action are less clear. Why could this action be bad? Why might it be good? Apply each of the Pope's five principles to this picture and respond to them.

6 Take the word 'ENVIRONMENT' and make your own acrostic poem to inspire people to care for the world around them.

7 Make a poster showing the reasons Christians are concerned about the environment and the reasons Humanists gave on pages 102–103.

Christians in conservation

A A Rocha's logo.

A ROCHA

Christians in Conservation

One Christian charity that is actively concerned with **conservation** is A Rocha. They began life in Britain in 1983 with the intention of showing God's love for all creation through conservation work. They say there are four good reasons why Christians should be involved in conservation work.

1 **LOVE** A Rocha says, 'Studying, thankfully enjoying and caring for the world that God has so wonderfully made is an obvious way for us to show our love for him.'

2 **OBEDIENCE** A Rocha says, 'If we desire to obey God, then we must look for ways in which we can be good and responsible **stewards** of the natural world.'

3 **JUSTICE** A Rocha says caring for the environment is part of justice because 'often it is the poor who suffer first when the environment is damaged'.

4 **HOPE** Although there is often depressing news about the damage we are causing to the environment, the Bible teaches hope because at some point in the future, it says, humanity and the environment will be in harmony.

1 Choose *one* of the four reasons above and explain more fully the Christian reasons for becoming involved in conservation work.

A Rocha describes itself as 'an international conservation organisation working to care for God's world' and map **B** shows where their current projects are located. You might like to learn more about some of these projects by consulting A Rocha's website.

Their first British project has been 'A Rocha Living Waterways' in Southall and Hayes in West London. In the middle of a heavily built-up multicultural area was 90 acres of wasteland. It had been used as a dump for burnt-out cars, fly-tipped waste and illegal motorbike scrambling. A Rocha launched a campaign to 'open up the wonders of God's creation to people who have little chance to enjoy the beauty of the natural world at first hand'.

Here is what their project includes:

- The transformation of a derelict 90-acre site into a country park and nature reserve, bringing green space to a cramped and overcrowded area.
- Environmental education through assemblies, after-school clubs and play schemes – helping form the attitudes of the next generation.
- A floating classroom on a purpose-built boat on the Grand Union Canal.
- A community newsletter in various languages, helping the religions locally to combine an agenda of creation care.
- A community environmental centre, acting as a focus for local people to come and find out about creation care and sustainable living.

C What ideas do you have for the regeneration of an area like this?

B A Rocha's projects.

FINLAND
CANADA
NETHERLANDS
UK
CZECH REPUBLIC
BULGARIA
FRANCE
LEBANON
USA
PORTUGAL
INDIA
PERU
GHANA
KENYA
SOUTH AFRICA

Activity

2 Go through each of the five parts of the project opposite and explain what people living in the area would gain from each one.

3 A Rocha says the different faith communities in the Southall area have welcomed the Living Waterways project 'and the common agenda of "creation care" is seen as an opportunity for building on shared values'.

   a What do they mean by 'creation care'?

   b Choose another religion and find out what their views are about caring for the planet.

4 Look at picture **C**. Prepare a double-sided A3 flier that could be distributed to houses in the neighbourhood encouraging a faith-based approach to regenerating the wasteland site.

Christian concern for animals

Christian groups hold different views about the way humans should treat animals. This is because the Bible does not give any precise guidance. In Genesis 1:26–28 (see page 104) it says God made humans in his image and put them in charge of the world. Three Christian groups below interpret this passage in different ways.

A Do you think Christians should be concerned about eating meat? Why?

The Church of England says:

'The value of animals has always been seen as secondary to that of human beings… In dealing with animals, Christians need to recognise they have a vested interest in controlling and regulating other species, and that this is part of the **divine** mandate [requirement] for responsible stewardship.'

The Quakers say:

'All animals should be treated as if they have rights and as if they suffer pain and stress similar to human experience and differing only in degree. We have a duty to consider the consequences of our influence on the environment and its effect on animals, taking great care to reduce the harmful effects. Some activities like killing for sport and aspects of trapping or hunting which involve cruelty in a slow death are indefensible.'

The Roman Catholic Church says:

'Roman Catholic moral theology would deny that animals have rights. Its teaching focuses, rather, on human duties towards animals, especially with regard to the right use of them… It is possible to oppose cruelty and exploitation without getting trapped in arguments about "rights"… Animals are not the equals of human beings, they do not have human rights, but on the other [hand] as part of God's creation they are owed respect and appropriate care.'

1 Imagine you are a Christian who is also the manager of the butchery department of a leading supermarket. Think about the following questions and write down your thoughts.

a Should you inform customers about the way the meat they are buying has been reared?

b Do you label the meat with information about welfare?

c Do you include a small picture of the animals being reared alongside the price label on the fixture?

d Do people just want cheap meat or do you think they care about how the animal has been treated?

e Would their reaction be different if the customers were Christian? Do you care about the way animals have been treated?

2 Sum up the differences of the three Christian denominations on these pages towards animals.

Situations vacant **B**

Due to expansion, **Silver Speed** requires experienced greyhound trainer for successful racing kennels. High salary and good working conditions for the right candidate. Apply Box 569.

Sasha, the nation's leading name in real fur, seeks trainee designer to work on this season's range of coats. Send full CV to Box 521.

Pets for Fun supermarket requires school leaver to train in general store work and care of the caged birds. Apply Box 681.

We are a pioneering research company looking for an experienced biochemist to work in our state-of-the-art animal laboratories. Experience in research into Alzheimer's disease would be an advantage. For further details apply to **JPZ** Box 226.

Mountways Bros require shift workers in the chicken-rearing house. No experience necessary. Apply Box 34.

Due to promotion, Anton's private zoo wishes to recruit a keeper for the sea lions. Willingness to work on the troupe's performance routine is essential. Apply Box 426.

3 a Using the situations vacant in **B**, make a list of the different ways in which people use animals.

b Are there any further ways you could add to the list?

4 a Would any jobs be unacceptable to Christians?

b Are there any jobs in **B** you would not like to do? Why?

5 Design a table, or use a spreadsheet, to analyse the different responses of the three Christian groups to the jobs described in **B**.

6 As a class, discuss: Animals don't have rights but we have responsibilities.

Religions united to care for the planet

objective

to look at an interfaith response to environmental concerns

glossary

Saint

Coming together to care for the planet

When Prince Philip was President of the World Wildlife Fund (WWF), he asked the different religions to meet together and discuss what they could do about the problems facing our planet. He said:

> If you believe in God – which is what Christians are supposed to do – then you should feel a responsibility to care for his creation.

He knew that all religions teach concern for the environment.

Assisi in Italy was chosen for the meeting because it is the birthplace of St Francis, a Christian **saint** well-known for his care of animals and his concern for the environment. The Assisi meeting also celebrated the 25th anniversary of WWF. It succeeded in getting members of several major world religions together along with people who held no religious beliefs. The aim of the conference was to see if they could work together to improve the environment.

Another meeting followed a few years later, by which time more religions had joined and the Alliance of Religions and Conservation was born – appropriately called ARC.

B ARC logo.

Today, ARC supports many environmental projects worldwide; some are quite small whilst others are on a very large scale. ARC is proof that religions can work together and united they can make a difference to the future of the planet.

One of their projects is called Sacred Land and reminds people 'that the landscape where they live can be as sacred as any holy island'. In Britain this has led to Christian, Hindu, Jewish, Muslim and secular communities working alongside each other to revive

A In 1986, representatives of some of the world's religions met in Assisi in Italy to discuss what they could do about the problems that faced the planet.

inner-city areas and create a community garden. Other projects have involved conserving and celebrating holy wells; rediscovering and renewing pilgrimage trails; protecting trees and woodlands; and celebrating sacred places with works of art or poems.

1 a **List each of the different projects mentioned above and write alongside what advantage you think each might have for a Christian.**

   b **Consider whether a Humanist might gain anything from involvement in one of these projects.**

Activity

ARC helped fund the garden at Pennant Melangell in Wales as part of ARC's Sacred Land project. The Cancer Help Centre at Pennant Melangell needed a Quiet Garden, somewhere beautiful and peaceful for people they counsel to sit in quiet reflection either on their own, or with family and friends.

C Pennant Melangell's garden. This is a very small project ARC worked on in Wales.

A group of nuns belonging to the Orthodox Monastery of the Protection of the Mother of God took over a derelict monastery near Avignon in France in 1992. They used traditional methods and local craftspeople to help them restore the buildings. There were also 60 hectares of land with the monastery but much of it had suffered from unmanaged grazing. In a massive

D On a much larger scale, ARC worked to reforest an ancient monastic site at Mas de Solan in France to enable the nuns to work the land in the traditional way.

reforestation project, ARC helped the nuns to introduce native trees and restore the site's natural habitats. Today, they are able to farm it in the traditional way which is sympathetic to the environment. They produce jams, cheeses, olive oil, vegetables and wines from their land. The head of the community, Mother Paissa, said, 'The land here is rich in flora and fauna, and particularly birds. We have no wish to change this. At Solan we want to create a natural sanctuary where animals can live free from danger.'

2 a **Think of a run-down area in your locality that might benefit from regeneration.**

   b **Plan a bid to ARC for funding for its regeneration. You will need to:**

   ● **give a brief description of the present state of the area**

   ● **state what you would like to see done, with sketches if necessary (pages 106–107 will remind you what A Rocha did in Southall)**

   ● **justify the cost, showing that many different groups in the community could benefit from the project**

   ● **explain why a Christian would support this work.**

Activity

objective

to think about how religions can co-operate in caring for the environment

glossary

Baha'i
Jainism
Soul

The lungs of the planet – concern for trees

Trees have been called 'the lungs of the planet' because they continually recycle carbon dioxide into oxygen. Ask for help from the geography and biology departments to find evidence that could back this statement. What problems are caused when trees are cut down and not replaced? Make a poster that shows a tree losing its leaves. On each leaf write a short piece of information about the problems of deforestation.

The Jains are working on a reforestation project in India to cut pollution. Under the slogan of 'one child one tree' they are planting trees in open plains and empty land around temples and schools, at the rate of 15–30,000 saplings a year. Many of the trees are fruit trees which will benefit the local economy.

A very ancient religion, **Jainism**, believes there is an immortal and indestructible **soul** in every living being. This means a Jain is concerned not to harm any living creature, no matter how tiny. Followers of the religion do not eat meat and many will eat only the leaves and fruits of a plant because if you eat the root, you kill it. The religion teaches that all of nature is bound together. If you don't care for nature, then you do not care for yourself, they say.

Activity

1 a Can you think of an example where caring for one part of the environment will actually care for humans?

 b Conversely, is there an example of harming the planet which will also harm humanity?

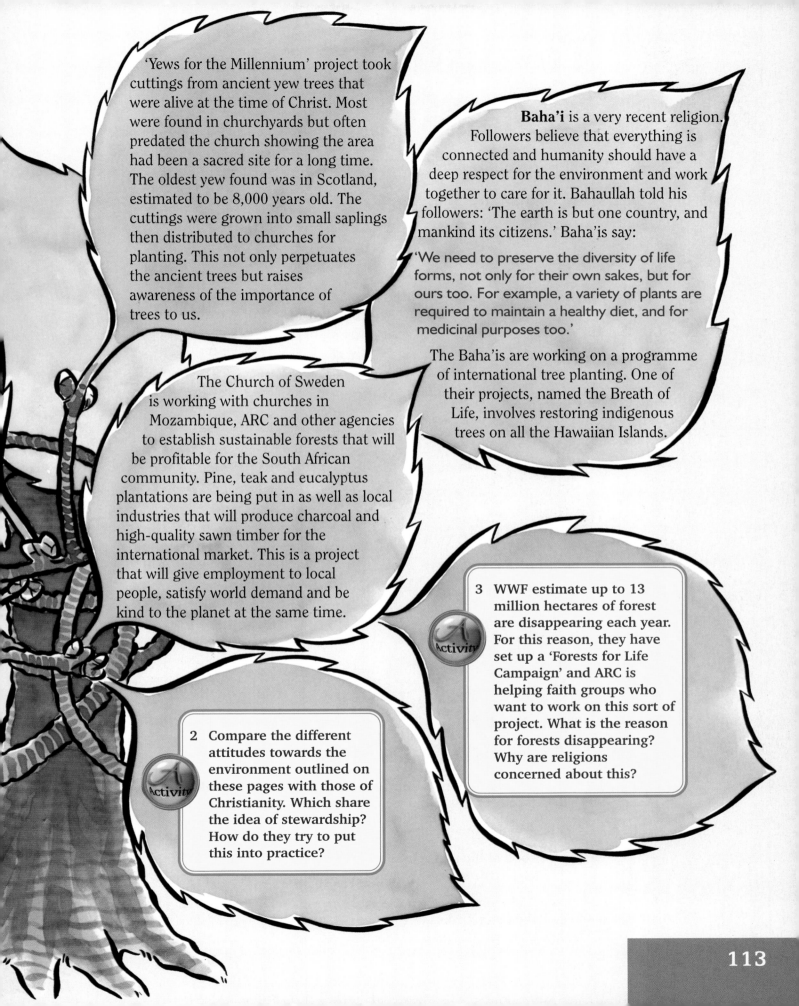

'Yews for the Millennium' project took cuttings from ancient yew trees that were alive at the time of Christ. Most were found in churchyards but often predated the church showing the area had been a sacred site for a long time. The oldest yew found was in Scotland, estimated to be 8,000 years old. The cuttings were grown into small saplings then distributed to churches for planting. This not only perpetuates the ancient trees but raises awareness of the importance of trees to us.

Baha'i is a very recent religion. Followers believe that everything is connected and humanity should have a deep respect for the environment and work together to care for it. Bahaullah told his followers: 'The earth is but one country, and mankind its citizens.' Baha'is say:

'We need to preserve the diversity of life forms, not only for their own sakes, but for ours too. For example, a variety of plants are required to maintain a healthy diet, and for medicinal purposes too.'

The Baha'is are working on a programme of international tree planting. One of their projects, named the Breath of Life, involves restoring indigenous trees on all the Hawaiian Islands.

The Church of Sweden is working with churches in Mozambique, ARC and other agencies to establish sustainable forests that will be profitable for the South African community. Pine, teak and eucalyptus plantations are being put in as well as local industries that will produce charcoal and high-quality sawn timber for the international market. This is a project that will give employment to local people, satisfy world demand and be kind to the planet at the same time.

2 Compare the different attitudes towards the environment outlined on these pages with those of Christianity. Which share the idea of stewardship? How do they try to put this into practice?

3 WWF estimate up to 13 million hectares of forest are disappearing each year. For this reason, they have set up a 'Forests for Life Campaign' and ARC is helping faith groups who want to work on this sort of project. What is the reason for forests disappearing? Why are religions concerned about this?

To fight or not to fight

objective

to open up the
debate about
conflict

War is an efficient way of solving a dispute. Soldiers are professional people who have freely chosen to do that job. They know the risks. And weapons are extremely sophisticated these days ensuring targets are hit with 'military precision'.
I know you are going to ask me about weapons of mass destruction (WMDs). Yes, well I'm all in favour of them. It's been the presence of WMDs that have kept world peace for so long. Everybody knows that if a nuclear war started it would wipe us all out, so nobody is prepared to start a world war.
Hey presto! Peace!

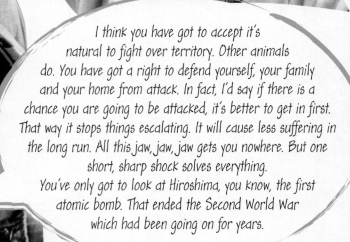

I think you have got to accept it's natural to fight over territory. Other animals do. You have got a right to defend yourself, your family and your home from attack. In fact, I'd say if there is a chance you are going to be attacked, it's better to get in first. That way it stops things escalating. It will cause less suffering in the long run. All this jaw, jaw, jaw gets you nowhere. But one short, sharp shock solves everything.
You've only got to look at Hiroshima, you know, the first atomic bomb. That ended the Second World War which had been going on for years.

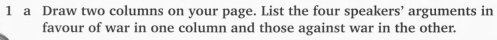

1 a **Draw two columns on your page. List the four speakers' arguments in favour of war in one column and those against war in the other.**

   b **Add any other points you can think of to either column.**

   c **Look at the two columns, then write down which side of the argument you agree with. Explain which argument is most significant for you.**

   d **Add the points from the other speech bubbles scattered on page 115 to the correct column.**

How can you say conflict is natural and right? I agree animals will fight to the death, but come on; it is our intelligence that makes us superior to the animal kingdom. We possess the power of reasoning. We don't need to resort to violence every time we have a disagreement. We can talk and work out a solution. Billions of pounds are spent annually on weapons that could be better spent eradicating poverty and removing the cause of many wars. 'Military precision' you say? Well, tell me what you mean by 'friendly fire'?

You can't say there are any real winners in a war. War is very destructive and I don't just mean the soldiers who get killed. Civilian lives are ruined. People's homes are destroyed, families get broken up and there is widespread suffering. War destroys the environment too. Look at the area around Hiroshima and Nagasaki. It has been poisoned for generations to come. Conventional wars destroy vegetation, crops and animals, not to mention huge numbers of civilians. So much for your sophisticated weapons.

For the cost of one jet fighter, three million children could be vaccinated against disease.

For evil to win, one good person just has to do nothing.

In the First World War, 95% of those killed were soldiers. In the Second World War, 16 million soldiers and 39 million civilians were killed. In recent wars, 90% of people killed were civilians.

Get it in proportion! Almost nine million died in the First World War but the flu epidemic of 1918 killed over 20 million.

War and conflict have a direct impact on development. Countries buy weapons with money needed for health, education or agriculture.

Every gun that is made, every warship launched, every rocket fired, signifies in a final sense, a theft from those who hunger and are not fed.

(President Eisenhower of the USA)

Activity

2 Take *one* of the points of view raised on these pages and write an argument against it.

3 Do you think Christians should get involved in these sorts of disputes? Why?

Is Christianity a peaceful religion?

to examine the evidence and decide what Christian teachings about conflict mean

You are the investigating judge!

People often want to know what Christians are supposed to do about conflict. This ranges from personal disagreements with people right through to going into battle. You are going to examine the evidence in order to come up with the answer.

A Do you think Christians should get involved in this sort of activity? Why?

Evidence from the Old Testament scriptures:

The evidence

In order to be as authoritative as possible, the evidence will be taken from the Bible. Some of it will come from the Old Testament, which are scriptures Jesus knew and used. Other evidence will be taken from what Jesus said and how he acted.

Good luck!

'He [God] will settle disputes among the nations,
among the great powers near and far.
They will hammer their swords into ploughs
and their spears into pruning knives.
Nations will never again go to war,
never prepare for battle again.'

(Micah 4:3)

'Do not commit murder.'

(Exodus 20:13)

'The Israelites killed every one of the enemy in the barren country where they had chased them. Then they went back to Ai and killed everyone there. Joshua kept his spear pointed at Ai and did not put it down until every person there had been killed. The whole population of Ai was killed that day – 12,000 men and women.'

(Joshua 8:24–26)

'He sets the time for love and the time for hate,
the time for war and the time for peace.'

(Ecclesiastes 3:8)

What Jesus actually said:

'Happy are those who work for peace; God will call them his children!'

(Matthew 5:9)

'You have heard that it was said, "An eye for an eye, and a tooth for a tooth." But now I tell you: do not take revenge on someone who wrongs you. If anyone slaps you on the right cheek, let him slap your left cheek too.'

(Matthew 5:38–39)

'Peace is what I leave with you; it is my own peace that I give you.'

(John 14:27)

'…love your enemies and pray for those who persecute you.'

(Matthew 5:43)

'…Whoever has a purse or a bag must take it; and whoever has no sword must sell his coat and buy one.'

(Luke 22:36)

What Jesus did:

Luke 22:36 is part of the instructions Jesus gave his followers not long before his death. By telling them to arm themselves, Jesus was accepting that his followers should fight to defend themselves.

- When Jesus went into the Temple in Jerusalem, he reacted furiously to the trade that was going on in the precincts:

'So he made a whip from cords and drove all the animals out of the Temple, both the sheep and the cattle; he overturned the tables of the moneychangers and scattered their coins; and he ordered those who sold the pigeons, "Take them out of here!"'

(John 2:15–16)

- Jesus' followers went into a village to find somewhere for Jesus to stay but the villagers would not have him. Jesus' followers returned to Jesus and said:

'…"Lord, do you want us to call fire down from heaven to destroy them?" Jesus turned and rebuked them.'

(Luke 9:54)

- When Jesus was arrested, one of his followers took out his sword and cut off the ear of the High Priest's servant. Jesus condemned the action:

'Put your sword back in its place… All who take the sword will die by the sword.'

(Matthew 26:52)

- After his arrest, Jesus was accused

'of many things, so Pilate questioned him again, "Aren't you going to answer? Listen to all their accusations."

Again Jesus refused to say a word, and Pilate was amazed.'

(Mark 15:3–5)

Throughout his trial, torture and execution, Jesus accepted his treatment and never retaliated in any way.

Activity

1 a Divide your page in two. Label one side 'In favour' and the other 'Against'.

b Read each extract and decide which column it should go in then enter the biblical reference with a brief note to remind yourself of the argument.

c When you have completed this, you need to pass judgement on the question at the beginning of this topic: 'Is Christianity a peaceful religion?' Write down your judgement and give a brief explanation for the reasons why you arrived at this decision. You should mention whether it was an easy decision to reach or whether there were any conflicting arguments.

2 Jesus is often referred to as the 'Prince of Peace'. Do you think this is an accurate title?

What do people think about war?

objective
to examine different views about war

glossary
Chaplain
Padre

Is it easier to go to war if you don't believe in God?

Some people might say if you don't believe in God, then war is fine. If you kill somebody deliberately, or accidentally, it won't matter because you won't get punished in the next life – there isn't one! But the Humanists, who do not believe in God or life after death, say this life is all the more precious. For that reason, they try to make the most of it and would think hard before supporting war. Humanists do agree, however, that it is not always easy to find a peaceful solution to some conflicts and it is possible that war may be the only option.

A Bertrand Russell was a well-known Humanist who campaigned against weapons of mass destruction. However, during the Second World War he agreed that war was morally justified.

Is it always wrong to kill somebody?

Christians and non-Christians agree that it is wrong to kill innocent people. The law in most countries would class this as murder and people have no difficulty in agreeing with this. For many people, the idea of killing someone in self-defence is different but, again, most people accept that it is justified.

Killing people in time of war can raise rather more questions, especially if a city is bombed and lots of innocent people are killed. Is it wrong to target civilians in a war, or are they fair game? Modern warfare includes weapons of mass destruction like biological and chemical weapons and nuclear bombs, which could kill millions of people if used.

- Does this affect your opinion of whether war is moral or immoral?
- Do you think there are situations where discussion breaks down and conflict is inevitable?

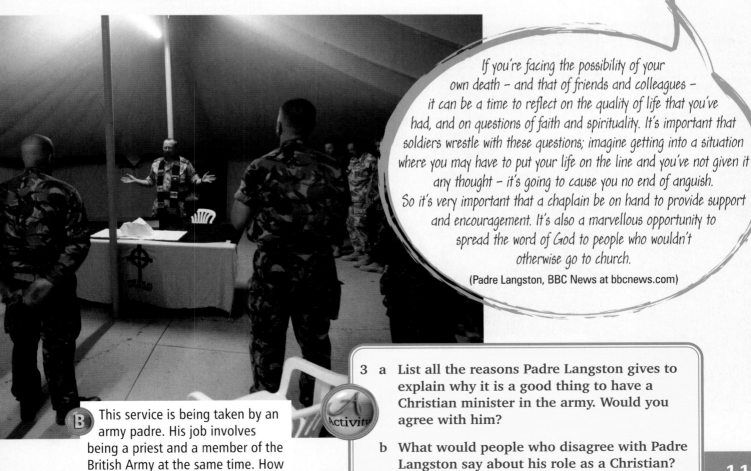

A man of God or a man of war?

Clinton Langston is an unusual Christian because he is a priest and a member of the British Army. He is an army **chaplain**, or **padre** as they are called. It might seem strange to many people that a priest could be actively involved in warfare, travelling with the regiment to whatever war zone they are posted to.

> *Joining the Army was not an easy decision for me; I did have to go through a lot of soul-searching. But I feel that in this imperfect world of ours, there comes a point when diplomacy fails because people don't listen.*
>
> (Padre Langston, BBC News at bbcnews.com)

He does wear camouflage uniform but does not carry a weapon because he is a man of peace.

Padre Langston says his job in the army is not to help with the conflict but to help the people who are caught up in war. Not only does he run services every Sunday, but he has time to spend with soldiers who are away from home and may be in great danger.

> *If you're facing the possibility of your own death – and that of friends and colleagues – it can be a time to reflect on the quality of life that you've had, and on questions of faith and spirituality. It's important that soldiers wrestle with these questions; imagine getting into a situation where you may have to put your life on the line and you've not given it any thought – it's going to cause you no end of anguish. So it's very important that a chaplain be on hand to provide support and encouragement. It's also a marvellous opportunity to spread the word of God to people who wouldn't otherwise go to church.*
>
> (Padre Langston, BBC News at bbcnews.com)

B This service is being taken by an army padre. His job involves being a priest and a member of the British Army at the same time. How could he help soldiers?

Activity

1 a Some people say religious differences cause most wars. Test this by looking through a few copies of national newspapers. Find out what conflicts are taking place around the world at the moment. How many of these are connected with religion?

b Did religion play a large part in the two World Wars of the twentieth century?

c Write down your own conclusion about the part religion plays in conflict.

2 Do you think people's attitude to war is affected by whether they believe in God and a life after death? Why?

Activity

3 a List all the reasons Padre Langston gives to explain why it is a good thing to have a Christian minister in the army. Would you agree with him?

b What would people who disagree with Padre Langston say about his role as a Christian?

objective

to understand the variation in Christian attitudes towards war

glossary

Just War
Pacifist
Quaker
Reconciliation
Spiritual

Although war is something most Christians would prefer did not happen, many believe there are occasions when war is the only way to defeat evil. To do nothing, they argue, allows evil to flourish. Many would quote the example of Hitler in the Second World War. Others might mention more recent examples of dictators like Idi Amin or Saddam Hussein who perpetrated terrible human rights abuses. There are occasions when war is just, some Christians say, and these are the criteria.

A Just War

1 There must be a just cause, e.g. self-defence.
2 It must be started by a proper authority, e.g. a government or ruler, not by an individual.
3 The war must be fought to bring about good. Once that has been achieved, fighting must stop and peace and justice be restored again.
4 War must be a last resort. Other methods, like negotiation, must have been tried.
5 War must be carried out in a just way, using only enough force to achieve your aim. Innocent civilians must be protected.

Some Christians have added another point saying you can only go to war if you stand a chance of succeeding. They say it is wrong to send troops to fight a hopeless cause.

Another person said people should weigh up whether the good achieved would outweigh the evil that caused the war.

A In 1963, Pope John XXIII said, 'It is impossible to conceive of a Just War in a nuclear age.' Would you agree with him? Why?

 Activity

1 Write each of the *five* points and the *two* additional ones describing a Just War on separate slips of paper. With a partner, arrange them in a pyramid shape with the point you consider most important at the top.

2 Choose a recent major conflict and apply each of the Just War criteria to it. Did it rank as a Just War? Do you think the conflict was justified?

3 With a partner, draw up your own list of rules that a country must consider before going to war. If you do not agree with war at all, simply design rules like 'Nobody must be injured', etc.

The Church of England has developed its own modern version of the **Just War**.

1 The war must be a defensive response to unjust aggression.
2 There must be a realistic chance of success.
3 There must be some proportion between the costs and the post-war settlement.
4 Only military targets can be chosen.
5 Force must never be an end in itself.

Quakers

There are other Christians who believe that war is never justified. Most Christian denominations have people within them who are **pacifist**, but only the **Quakers** are totally pacifist and have been throughout their 300-year-old history. An early Quaker said in 1693, 'A good end cannot sanctify evil means; nor must we ever do evil, that good may come of it.' What does this mean?

They argue that violence is not an effective way of combating evil. By believing there is 'that of God in everyone', Quakers think more can be achieved by appealing to a person's capacity for love and goodness, than by using punishment or retaliation. '**Spiritual** weapons – love, truth-saying, non-violence, imagination and laughter – are weapons that heal and do not destroy.'

B Quakers are one of the few Christian groups that believe in pacifism. They argue that violence never achieves anything. They argue for negotiation every time. What do you think?

Quaker pacifism does not mean doing nothing in time of war. During the Second World War when there was conscription, Quakers worked as stretcher-bearers or in medical teams. Today, they work behind the international scene to promote peace, assist with mediation at the United Nations and campaign for nuclear disarmament.

Roman Catholic Church

The Roman Catholic Church has spoken out against nuclear weapons on several occasions. Whilst understanding that there is a case for nuclear weapons being a deterrent, they have been concerned that these weapons can be aimed 'indiscriminately against large cities along with the population' and that is regarded as 'a crime against God and man'.

CAFOD, the Catholic charity that helps with overseas development, says:

War and conflict have a direct impact on development. In times of war crops are destroyed, or people may be forced to leave their homes before they can plant or harvest their crops. Millions of people flee areas where there is fighting to look for safety. Anti-personnel landmines make land unusable. Roads and bridges are destroyed, schools and health clinics closed.

As a result, CAFOD has been working on programmes focused on **reconciliation** and peace-building, as well as campaigning for a ban on landmines.

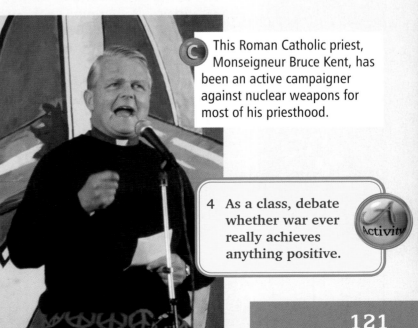

C This Roman Catholic priest, Monseigneur Bruce Kent, has been an active campaigner against nuclear weapons for most of his priesthood.

4 As a class, debate whether war ever really achieves anything positive.

Activity

CHIPS

CHIPS = Christian International Peace Service

CHIPS was started 40 years ago in response to conflict between the communities in Cyprus. Since then, it has worked in India, the Philippines, Northern Ireland and even inner-city London to help communities live together in peace.

> 1 a Read the leaflet in **A** and write down where CHIPS is currently working.
>
>   b Make a list of the things CHIPS is helping the people to do and decide how these projects might bring peace between the Karamojong and Iteso tribes.
>
> 2 Underneath their name, CHIPS often puts the quotation from Matthew's Gospel 5:9 when Jesus said, 'Happy are those who work for peace; God will call them his children.' Look back at the Christian teachings about conflict on pages 116–117 and decide which ones CHIPS members are trying to follow.

CHIPS says its aim is to work 'for peace and reconciliation in areas of conflict and tension, through **Jesus** Christ who is our Peace'. They work with people from all branches of Christianity to achieve world peace.

To put this into practice, members of the CHIPS team live in the communities where there are conflicts. They share the same housing, eat the traditional foods, learn the language and share in all aspects of local life. This is to give them a good understanding of the people, their lifestyle, culture, skills and problems. CHIPS members live amongst people on both sides of the conflict. It is because of the close relationships they form that reconciliation is possible.

CHIPS is very 'hands-on', working with members of the community on practical projects that will reduce poverty. Helping to reduce poverty sows seeds of peace and helps to establish good relationships. For example, it has been the lack of clean water and cattle theft in one area of Uganda that have been the main causes of conflict between two tribes. The CHIPS team made 46 hand-dug wells and assisted with the repair and building of dams. This made a huge difference to the communities. Firstly, their people were employed working on the dams and then, when those were completed, the tribes were able to bring their cattle to drink. At one dam alone between 300 and 500 head of cattle visit every day to drink.

> 3 Some people say that making peace isn't enough. What is needed is to remove the cause of the conflict in the first place. What do you think CHIPS' attitude to this would be and what is the evidence?

Road rehabilitation, Uganda

PRACTICAL PROJECTS

The team work together with the local community to improve their livelihood and encourage co-operation between opposing groups. The team empowers the community to fulfil their emerging hopes.

UGANDA

CHIPS is currently working in N.E.Uganda to reconcile the tribes of the Karamojong and Iteso. Projects in Uganda have included: agricultural initiatives; well-digging and rehabilitation of cattle dams; tree planting; veterinary care; road rehabilitation; and the re-settlement of abandoned areas.

CHIPS is a small specialist organisation which works for peace and reconciliation in areas of conflict and tension, through Jesus Christ who is our Peace.

Small teams of Christians, including members from both sides of a conflict and from abroad, live together in the area of tension, at the economic level of the people they are helping.

They work alongside the local population to implement practical projects, encouraging opposing sides to work together to remove the poverty caused by conflict.

The team absorb the enmity from both sides, sharing the Gospel of reconciliation through Christ, serving the communities both practically and spiritually.

PEACE PLACE

WORKING FOR PEACE IN AREAS OF CONFLICT AND TENSION

Karamojong warriors display their weapons

CHIPS
Christian International Peace Service

The inspiration of Jesus

CHIPS works in a quiet way drawing inspiration from the life and teachings of Jesus Christ. Jesus lived quietly with his family in their community for most of his life. He treated everyone as equal and helped people others had rejected. At the end of his life when he was tortured and crucified, Jesus accepted the accusations and abuse that were thrown at him, becoming the scapegoat for all the hatred that was around.

As part of the peacemaking, CHIPS' members listen to people's anger and hatred. By doing this they allow people to 'get it off their chest'. It is CHIPS' members who absorb the hatred and channel it away. As Christians, they are able to turn to God in **prayer** to support them.

Activity

4 How does CHIPS try to prevent conflict and also defuse conflict?

5 Read their leaflet in **A**, then write an advert for someone to train as a CHIPS team member for Uganda.

Working for world peace

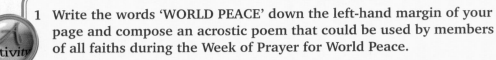

1 Write the words 'WORLD PEACE' down the left-hand margin of your page and compose an acrostic poem that could be used by members of all faiths during the Week of Prayer for World Peace.

2 Read the list of organisations in box **C** who were associated with the Week of Prayer for World Peace.

a List the different religions involved in these organisations.

b Make a list of the non-religious groups involved.

c Choose *two* organisations that you know nothing about to research further. The Internet is always a good place to start.

> The peace of the world needs to be prayed for by the faiths of the world.
>
> (Edward Carpenter)

A Logo of the Week of Prayer for World Peace.

The International Prayer for Peace

Lead me from death to life, from falsehood to truth,
Lead me from despair to hope, from fear to trust.
Lead me from hate to love, from war to peace.
Let peace fill our heart, our world, our universe.

B

C

Some organisations associated with the Week of Prayer for World Peace
Anglican Pacifist Fellowship
Anglican Society for the Welfare of Animals
Bharatiya-Vidya Bhavan
Brahma Kumaris
Buddhist Society
Campaign against the Arms Trade
Centre for the Study of Islam and Christian-Muslim relations
Christian Aid
Christian CND
Christian Peace Conference UK
Churches Commission on Interfaith Relations

Conscience – the Peace Tax Campaign
Fellowship Party
Fellowship of Reconciliation
Gandhi Foundation
Justice and Peace Commission
Muslim Association for Teaching Humility, Equality, Morals, Altruism, Tolerance, Integration and Community Services
National Council of Hindu Temples UK
National Spiritual Assembly of the Baha'is of the UK
Nipponzan Myohoji
Northern Friends Peace Board
One World Week
Oxfam
Pax Christi

Quaker Peace and Social Witness
Quaker Universalist Group
Rissho Kosei-kai
Roman Catholic Committee for Other Faiths
Schumacher Society
Three Faiths Forum
Toc H
Unitarian Peace Fellowship
United Nations Association
Women's International League for Peace and Freedom
World Conference of Religions for Peace
World Congress of Faiths
World Disarmament Campaign
World Peace Flame Project
World Peace Prayer Society

The list in box **C** shows that most religions believe there is much to gain when all religions co-operate. The Week of Prayer was launched with representatives from all faiths gathering for prayers at Westminster Abbey. When members of the faiths returned to their own places of worship, they took with them a leaflet of prayers they could use for the rest of the week. The difference was that they would be using prayers from other religions in their worship. Look at the prayers recommended for Day One in **D**. The theme that day was 'Forgiveness and Reconciliation'.

D

Day One

'Refrain from anger and forsake wrath.'

(Psalm 3:8 Hebrew Bible and Old Testament)

'Do not fear
He who fears, hates;
He who hates, kills;
Break your sword and throw it away.'

(Hindu, Ghandi)

'We pray for:
- those who have been tragically wounded
- people who are taught bitterness towards others
- nations and individuals with scores to settle
- those who cannot allow themselves to forgive
- those who are unable to let themselves be forgiven.

May peace triumph over discord.'

(Zoroastrian)

'Allah does not change a people's lot unless they change what is in their hearts.'

(Qur'an 13)

'Forgive us the wrongs we have done, as we forgive the wrongs that others have done to us.'

(Matthew 6:12)

Respect for all

In Bradford, where people of many religions live alongside each other, a twinning project has begun. Some schools have chosen to partner with a school that has a totally different background to theirs. One school with a largely white Christian school population twinned with another where pupils came from a multicultural background.

The aim of the project has been for teachers, pupils and parents to learn more about each other's religions and cultures. RE lessons have often provided the perfect opportunity for schools to co-operate.

Pupils in one school made a DVD in class to introduce themselves to a class in the other school. It was exciting when they received the DVD from their twin and heard about the interests of pupils in that school. This led to e-mail-pals and work on the same material in RE. Imagine how useful it is to be able to e-mail an expert for help with your homework on their place of worship! It was fun too when the e-mail-pals met up and were able to go on joint school visits to places of worship. Each was able to guide the other around their place of worship and answer their questions.

3 If you were planning a twinning project for your school, what would you like people to gain from the experience? What type of school would you suggest they twinned with? Suggest some activities that your class and the fellow-class could work on together. What do you think of the idea?

E School twinning projects have turned out to be great fun as well as educational.

Assessment for Unit 3

'When I look at the sky, which you have made,
at the moon and the stars, which you set in their places –
what are human beings, that you think of them;
mere mortals, that you care for them?

Yet you made them inferior only to yourself;
you crowned them with glory and honour.
You appointed them rulers over everything you made;
you placed them over all creation:
sheep and cattle, and the wild animals too;
the birds and the fish and the creatures in the seas.'

(Psalm 8)

These questions test different sets of skills in RE. Which skills do you need to work on? Choose the level you need and work through the tasks set.

Level 3

- Read Psalm 8. Which part could a Christian quote to show God has given them the right to rule over animals? Do you think we have a right to use animals as we like? Why?
- Describe *two* different Christian responses to war. What would your reaction be if you were called up to fight? Why?
- Describe *three* ways Christians put Jesus' teachings about caring for the poor into action? What is your response to the person collecting for charity outside the supermarket? Why?

Level 4

- Describe what Christians mean when they speak of being 'stewards of the earth'. What difference could it make to the way they behave? Do you think it is worth doing? Why?
- Describe *two* different Christian attitudes towards war, explaining the reasons each uses to support their view. Do you agree with either of them? Why?
- Jesus said that whatever his followers did to help others, it was the same as if they had helped him. Explain how this has inspired charities like Christian Aid to act. Why do you think non-Christian organisations like Barnado's still want to help people?

Level 5

- What difference could it make to the welfare of the birds in the picture if the owner was a Christian? What biblical teachings would inspire him?
- Why might some Christians decide to be pacifists? Do you think this is acceptable or does everyone have a duty to fight for their country? Why?
- Explain what inspires some Christians to give up everything? The 20 richest people in the world own more than the 48 poorest countries in the world. Do you think anything should be done about this? Why?

Level 6

- Explain your reaction to those Christians who say there is nothing wrong with being very rich. Would you prefer they gave everything to the poor? Why?
- Explain why some Christians use Jesus' teachings to support war and others to support pacifism. What are the strengths and weaknesses of their arguments? Which do you agree with?
- What environmental challenges do you think Christians face if they take the words of the psalmist literally? Explain how the concept of stewardship fits in with this? Do you think a non-believer has any responsibility towards the environment? Why?

Glossary

Absolute poverty   Describes people who are so poor they struggle to survive.

Adult baptism   Ceremony where people are immersed in water to become members of the Christian Church.

Agnostic   Someone who is not sure whether there is a God or not.

Apparition   A vision of something paranormal, e.g. a ghost.

Atheist   Someone who does not believe that God exists.

Baha'i   A religion which began in Iran in the nineteenth century.

Baptism   A ceremony to welcome a Christian into membership.

Bible   The holy book of Christianity.

Big Bang   The theory that the universe began with a giant explosion.

Chaplain   A member of the Christian clergy who works in places like hospitals, prisons, the police or the military.

Civil wedding   A legal marriage that does not involve any religion.

Cohabiting   When a couple lives together without being married.

Coincidence   A chance happening.

Confirmation   A ceremony where a person commits to living a Christian life.

Conscience   The part of us which makes us aware of right and wrong.

Conservation   Looking after and protecting nature and natural resources.

Covenant   An agreement between God and the Jewish people.

Creationist   Someone who believes the world was created exactly as it is described in the Bible.

Crucifix   A cross symbolising where Jesus was crucified.

Darwin   Charles Darwin was the scientist credited with the Theory of Evolution.

Deforestation   The destruction of forests by cutting and burning.

Disciples   Followers of a teacher like Jesus.

Divine   Holy or godly.

Evangelical   A pro-active movement in the Christian Church.

Evolution   The theory that life on earth gradually developed over a long time.

Fair trade   Buying and selling goods at an honest price.

Free will   The idea that people can choose how they behave.

Global warming   The increase in the temperature of the earth's surface caused by the burning of fossil fuels and pollutants.

Gospels   The first four books of the New Testament: Matthew; Mark; Luke; and John which contain the life and teachings of Jesus.

Guardian angel   A spirit which watches over a person and protects them from harm.

Hallucination   An imaginary experience.

Holy Communion   A church service where people receive bread and wine in memory of Jesus, also known as the Eucharist or the Lord's supper.

Humanist   A group of people who believe humans, not God, are responsible for their own lives.

Icon   Image or representation of holy people used in the Orthodox Church.

Jainism   An ancient religion mainly practised in India which shares many beliefs with Buddhism and Hinduism.

Jesus   Believed by Christians to be the son of God. The founder of Christianity.

Just War   A war or conflict which is morally acceptable.

Kibbutz   A community of Jewish people where people share work and responsibilities.

Liturgy   A set form of prayer or church service.

Martyrdom   Giving your life for your beliefs.

Mass   The Roman Catholic form of Holy Communion.

Meditation   Thinking about something very deeply in silence and with deep concentration.

Methodist   A Christian denomination.

Miracle   Something which cannot be explained.

Missionary   Someone who is sent to spread the Christian faith.

New Testament   The second part of the Bible which contains the life of Jesus and the early Church.

Old Testament   The first part of the Bible which contains the history of the Jews and is the holy book for Jewish people.

Omnipotent   All powerful.

Omniscient   All knowing.

Orthodox Church   A branch of Christianity.

Pacifist   Someone who is against war and believes conflicts should be settled peacefully.

Padre   A member of the Christian clergy who works in the armed forces.

Pandemic   A global outbreak of a contagious disease, an epidemic on a massive scale.

Paranormal   Something supernatural which cannot be explained.

Prayer   A way of communicating with God.

Quaker   A Christian denomination.

Reconciliation   When two sides make friends again.

Redeem   To restore or save from sin.

Redemption   The belief that Jesus saves people from the consequences of their sins.

Reincarnation   The belief that when a person dies their soul is reborn into a new body.

Relative poverty   Where someone is not as rich as another person.

Resurrection   The belief that Jesus rose from death.

Revelation   An event caused by God.

Roman Catholic   The largest Christian denomination, led by the Pope.

Saint   Someone who has officially been recognised as a holy person.

Salvation Army   A Christian denomination.

Saviour   A title Christians give to Jesus because they believe that he saved people from their sins.

Soul   The part of a person which is eternal and independent of the body.

Soup Run   Organised by the Salvation Army to provide homeless people with a hot meal.

Spirit   The essence of a person.

Spiritual   A holy experience.

Steward   Someone who manages or looks after something for another.

Stewardship   The idea that humans look after the earth for God.

Supernatural   Something that does not exist in nature or cannot be explained.

Ten Commandments   The set of rules handed down by God to Moses thousands of years ago.

Transubstantiation   The Roman Catholic belief that during mass the bread and wine actually changes into the body and blood of Jesus.

Trinity   The Christian belief that God is made up of three 'parts' the Father, the Son and the Holy Spirit.

Tsunami   Tidal wave caused by the movement of the earth's crust in an earthquake or volcano.

Ultimate question   Questions about the meaning of life which do not have a right or wrong answer.

Unconditional love   Absolute, unlimited love given with 'no strings attached'.

Index